The Catalan Vengeance

The
Catalan Vengeance

Alfonso Lowe

Routledge & Kegan Paul
London and Boston

First published *1972*
by Routledge & Kegan Paul Ltd
Broadway House, 68–74 Carter Lane,
London EC4V 5EL and
9 Park Street, Boston, Mass. 02108, U.S.A.
Printed in Great Britain by
Ebenezer Baylis and Son, Ltd.,
The Trinity Press, Worcester, and London

ISBN 0 7100 7323 2

Contents

Illustrations

All the illustrations are from Archivo Mas, Barcelona. Plate 1 is
from a painting by Moreno Carbonero, in the Senate House,
Madrid. All the others are from the frescoes by José Maria Sert
y Badia, in the Hall of the Chronicles, the City Hall, Barcelona.

Preface

This is the story of one of the world's great adventures. Strangely enough, it is almost unknown to Anglo-American readers, though abbreviated accounts appear in a few history books from Gibbon onwards. Still more strangely, the whole story, from expedition to the extinction of the Catalan duchies in Greece, has never appeared as a monograph, even in Spain. The English translation of Muntaner's chronicle, which deals only with the first ten years of the venture, is in the limited edition of the Hakluyt Society and difficult to obtain.

No account of the murderous drama has been impartial; even though I have tried conscientiously, I have found it difficult to take the middle road between admiration for Spanish heroism and compassion for the unfortunate Greeks. The former recalls Xenophon's Ten Thousand and, even more, Pizarro's handful of adventurers; the Catalan Company, in fact, was the first to claim the title *conquistadores*.

Only once have I ventured far beyond the known facts, which are so exciting as to need no embellishment. That is in an attempt to account for Roger de Flor's visit to Adrianople, where he was murdered. No previous conjecture explains the incredible foolhardiness of an otherwise shrewd and careful adventurer. My guess is at least more plausible than Roger's own stated reason or those hazarded by the chroniclers. The motive for his murder is plain;

my tentative explanation of the means enables the reader to join me in an essay of detection.

Spelling of names is a recurrent problem. Should one write Peter or Pedro or Pere for a Catalan? Phocaea or Phokaia? I have followed no rigid rule, preferring to be guided by euphony and custom.

A.L.

Sitges, Barcelona

Prologue

For 500 years the Greek nursed a supreme malediction. He treasured it through the centuries of Turkish rule. If he survived their massacres and their slave traders he would wish it on his worst enemy. He did not call on Heaven to send down on him the bastinado, the scimitars of the Janissaries or the atrocities of the Bashi-Bazouks. In the last century it was still the ultimate curse in Thrace and even today its memory lingers: Ἡ ἐκδίκησις τῶν καταλάνων εὕροι σε 'May the Catalan Vengeance overtake you!'

Rome was mistress of the world. Growing old and feeling the approach of death, she did what some living organisms do—she reproduced herself by fission. The division was between east and west. When the latter went down to barbarian invasions, the former survived and transmitted to the west the wealth and wisdom of the east. From Constantinople the Eastern Empire, or Byzantium, controlled the trade of the Levant and beyond; to her came silk and spices from the east, perfumes from the south, furs and amber from the north. But wealth and power excite envy and her story is of one long battle against the 'have nots'. In the eighth century she repelled the Arabs with the use of her secret weapon, the Greek Fire; wild tribes pressed down from the north, Parthians from the east. Then the west, too, became jealous; Normans and Angevins in Sicily dreamed in turn of the conquest of Constantinople; and in the eleventh century Christendom's greatest menace, the Seljuk Turks, arrived in Asia Minor.

When the Turks captured the holy places of Palestine, they increased the dangers to western pilgrims visiting Jerusalem. The Byzantine Emperor Alexius I Comnenus possibly embellished the story, convinced that his own empire had no chance of recovering lost ground without the help of the west. By asking for aid he conjured up a demon that was eventually to swallow most of his empire, long before the Turks took it all. The first Crusaders carved out their fiefs in Syria and beyond, and tales of the wealth of Byzantium filtered back to hungry soldiers in western Europe. Wealth on one side and greed on the other led to mutual mistrust, amply justified on both sides.

The Turks, whose arrival was the catalyst for action by the west against Byzantium, were a collection of tribes seeking grazing grounds and a homeland and prepared to take them by force if the opposition was weak. The first wave, the Seljuks, appeared in Asia Minor in the eleventh century and in the single day of Manzikert made a mockery of Byzantium's armed might. They in turn became subject to the Mongols who had been started on their career of conquest, from China to Europe, by Genghis Khan. Now other Turkish tribes also moved westward; seven of them entered Anatolia, or Asia Minor, and one of them, the Ögrül, settled in the Sögüt region, south-east of Bursa. By 1300, in the period which concerns us, their leader Osman I, had begun to organize the tribe on military lines; they became the conquerors later known eponymously as the Osmanli or Ottoman Turks.

They were not yet the formidable fighters who would capture Constantinople and spread over the Balkans to the gates of Vienna; nor was their corps of 'storm troops', the Janissaries, due to be formed for another thirty years. But they were efficient enough to defeat Byzantine armies in the field. Still a tribe on the march, with all the impedimenta of Asiatic nomads, their chief strength lay in their bowmen and their cavalry, often combined as mounted archers. The Ottomans had one advantage over the stronger Turkish tribes to the south; they were the only group that still had unconquered Byzantine territory before it. For this reason they attracted a swarm of refugees, malcontents and adventurers, who increased their fighting potential. It was this horde which was menacing Constantinople in 1302, when our story opens.

But much had happened in the intervening 200 years. Pisans and Genoese had set up trading posts in the eastern Mediterranean, quickly followed by the Venetians. All became rich, but for the

Venetians the spoils of Constantinople were a greater and more compelling lure than the paltry gains of honest trade. They saw their chance about the year 1200 and the tale of how they used a religious enterprise for their own ends must be told in order to set the stage for the dramatic story of the Catalan Company.

The fourth Crusade was remarkable for two reasons: first, the whole army was excommunicated; and second, it captured two Christian cities and failed to encounter the Moslem infidels it had set out to fight.

From the beginning it was a business enterprise. Though Villehardouin speaks of those who took the Cross 'to avenge the shame done to Jesus Christ and to reconquer Jerusalem', most authorities agree that it was essentially an undertaking to satisfy personal ambition, land hunger and commercial aspirations. In 1198 the newly-elected Pope, Innocent III, instructed a fanatical priest of France, Fulk of Neuilly, to preach a Crusade and himself appropriated one-fortieth of clerical incomes to finance it. The first positive step was taken by some knights at a tournament in Ecri Castle, Champagne, in November 1199. Among the four knights who took the Cross it is interesting to read the name of Simon de Montfort, father of the rebellious baron who fought against our Henry III and was killed at Evesham. The movement spread through France, Burgundy and Flanders, and of the many who enrolled, Count Thibaut of Champagne and Brie (which sounds like a mid-morning snack) was elected leader.

The next four years were spent in recruiting and haggling. The latter was the result of a cunning manœuvre on the part of the Doge of Venice, Henry Dandolo; when the Crusaders were unable to produce the whole of the agreed passage money, he proposed to let them off their debt if they would help him reconquer the city of Zara (Zadar) in Illyria, recently taken by the Hungarians. The Pope threatened excommunication for those who attacked fellow Christians and implemented his threat when Zara was taken. Later the northerners were absolved, but the Venetians preferred to keep what they had won and risk the next world.

Meanwhile the fugitive Alexius (whose father, the Emperor Isaac II Angelus of Byzantium, had been deposed, blinded and imprisoned by his own brother, Alexius III) asked the Crusaders to help him reinstate his father. He offered commercial privileges to the Venetians, riches to other mercenary Crusaders and assistance

3

against the Turks to the idealists. Innocent III forbade the attack on Constantinople, so they proceeded with it, except for a few who followed Simon de Montfort and sailed for Syria.

When Thibaut of Champagne died in 1201 the Crusaders elected Boniface of Montferrat as his successor. Our outline has to pass over the siege of Constantinople, the restoration of Alexius, his murder and the subsequent capture, burning and looting of Constantinople by the Crusaders. In accordance with their agreement, a treaty of partition was drawn up. All thought of war against the Turks had been put aside; the Venetians concentrated on the commercial, the Franks on their territorial ambitions.

Count Baldwin (Baudouin) of Flanders was elected first Latin Emperor of Constantinople and given a quarter of the loot. The remaining three-quarters were divided equally between the Venetians and the other Crusaders. Thus the former were able to style themselves (a claim that has puzzled many) rulers of a quarter and half a quarter (i.e. three-eighths) of the 'Empire of Romania', as the Byzantines had called it. Partitioning among the Franks followed the usual feudal pattern: Boniface of Montferrat—perhaps as recompense for not receiving the sceptre—was made King of Salonika and immediately marched to conquer his new lands. He met with no opposition, for he was popular with the Greeks and had married the widow of Isaac II. He was accompanied by a host of needy Crusaders, eager for the fiefs they expected him to bestow. Among them were Othon de la Roche, a Burgundian of noble blood, and the brothers Jacques and Nicholas of St Omer, nephews of a Flemish knight. Between them they were to found the ruling families of Athens and Thebes, cities which figure so prominently in the story of the Catalan Company.

Thebes surrendered, as did the Acropolis of Athens; the Crusaders ruthlessly plundered the cathedral that occupied the Parthenon, oblivious to the associations of that monument. A hundred years later the Catalans sacked Thebes and their deed was remembered long after the Crusaders' treatment of Athens was forgotten.

The Morea, as the Peloponnese was now called, was invaded by Boniface in spite of the resistance of a Greek noble, the 'Lasgur' of Frankish chronicles; he was Leon Sgouros, Lord of Nauplia, Argos and Corinth. Geoffrey de Villehardouin the chronicler, hearing of the outcome of the fourth Crusade, left Syria for Constantinople. A storm blew him to Modon, where a Greek traitor invited him to join in a career of conquest.* They cut their way through to Boniface, who was besieging Nauplia, obtained his approval, conquered the Morea and founded the long line of the Princes of Achaia, patrons of chivalry.

The practical Venetians were less concerned with territorial gains than with the establishment of a chain of trading posts extending from Italy to the Levant. They acquired, either by the treaty of partition, by purchase or by force of arms, the islands of Corfu, Zante, Cephalonia, Cythera, Crete, the greater part of Euboea (Negroponte), the Cyclades and many Aegean Islands. But their most useful acquisitions were the ports of Modon and Coron in Messenia. Thus the fourth Crusade, thanks to the foresight of old Henry Dandolo, established Venice as the greatest trading power in the Levant.

Of the Byzantine rulers, Isaac II became a puppet emperor for a few months, associated with his son Alexius IV. The latter's generous promises to the Crusaders proved too expensive; the exasperated citizens deposed him and elected a kinsman, Alexius V Ducas, usually known as Mourzophles because his eyebrows met in the mid-line. He, too, lasted only a short time and was executed by the Crusaders, after being blinded by the Greeks.

Three Byzantine areas remained independent, waiting for the day when the strength of the Latins would diminish. It was generally assumed that the largest, that of Nicaea in Asia Minor, was the logical heir to the fallen Angelus dynasty. There the Lascaris descendants survived, thanks to the intelligent use of war and marriage, until in 1258 the founder's great-grandson, John IV, became nominal ruler at the age of seven and a half. Three years later he had lost his empire to an efficient and ambitious relative, Michael Palaeologos. The time was now ripe for the recovery of Constantinople, which was regained from the degenerate descendants of the Crusaders without a fight. The child John lost more than Nicaea; with the ruthless barbarity that characterized the eastern heirs of Rome, the usurper had him blinded; remember this when you read of Catalan atrocities towards Byzantine Greeks. With the unfortunate child now unfit to rule, the Genoese bound to him by a treaty and the Latins disappearing rapidly, Michael had only to cross the Bosphorus to gain a throne.

He recovered Constantinople in 1261 and found it bankrupt,

---

* The chronicler must not be confused with his uncle, Geoffrey de Villehardouin, marshal of Champagne and Romania.

neglected and surrounded by enemies. Grass grew in the streets and large areas of the formerly populous city were deserted. The gold coinage, for centuries the only stable one in Europe, was well on the road to debasement in a vain attempt to catch up with insolvency. Makeshifts of many kinds took the place of sound finance: unpaid tax gatherers extorted what they could from the peasants and throve on what remained after handing in their quota. Forced contributions and an increase in the normal degree of corruption fought a losing battle against extravagance and further dishonesty. But amid the threats of military and financial collapse the court of Michael VIII, as he was now called, relaxed hardly a detail of the rigid, oriental formality that Byzantium had maintained for so many centuries. And so it continued under his son Andronicus II and the co-Emperor, his grandson Michael IX.[1]

In Greece, the Frankish barons were not intimidated as easily as their relations the Latin rulers in Constantinople. They remained in possession of Athens, Thebes, the Morea and such islands as the Venetians did not need for another half century. Their eventual fate is bound up with that of the Catalan Company.

I have listed enemy nations that surrounded Byzantium. Of all foreigners the friendly Genoese were possibly the most objectionable; for one thing they were the nearest, with their own parish church and fortified watch-tower, on the far side of the Golden Horn. For another, they were as crafty as the Greeks and more efficient. They had gained a favoured position by helping Michael VIII and the Venetians had fallen out of favour proportionately, for their alliance with the Latin emperors and their part in the fourth Crusade. A 'most favoured nation' treaty had therefore placed the Genoese where no rival could compete with them, to the great annoyance of the Venetians. But they were necessary, and from this stemmed their unpopularity with the emperor.

The Catalans, like the Genoese and Venetians, were a nation of merchants and had been visitors to the near east since the eleventh century. By the end of the thirteenth they had established consulates in Egypt, Syria, Armenia, Persia and Constantinople, and were known throughout the Levant as pilgrims, Crusaders and merchants. Their light infantry, the Almugavars,[2] were the backbone of the Catalan Grand Company; we shall follow their fortunes from Sicily to the Iron Gates of Cilicia and back to Athens and it is as well to know how they came on the scene (see Appendix).

Chapter 1

The Company goes east 1302

In the autumn of the year 1302 the Catalan Grand Company set sail from Messina to save Byzantium from the Turks. Its livelihood was war and it comprised the most formidable infantry of the day, the dreaded Almugavars. Of these there were 4,000, accompanied by wives, mistresses and children, constant witnesses of their triumphs —or their shame. Contemporary writers assume, no doubt correctly, that the presence of their families was enough to banish any thought of retreat. This expedition differed from previous exploits in one important respect: formerly the Company had been a band of mercenary adventurers; now it was a tribe that sought a new home at the point of the sword. The emperors of Byzantium, their present employers, had as yet no suspicion of this.

The men were mainly Catalans and Aragonese from the northeast of Spain, differing in language, but neighbours on land and subjects of the same king, James II of Aragón. They had fought for him and his father, Peter III, in North Africa and in the defence of Sicily against Charles of Anjou.* As explained in the Appendix, their support of Frederick II of Sicily against his brother James II was regarded as treason and prevented their return to Spain. But adventure, double wages and the hope of booty called them eastward as strongly as their reluctance to go home.

The Etesian wind was blowing from the north-west and the fleet made a quick passage to Monemvasia, the strongest fortress in the

* See Appendix.

Morea. A welcome awaited them, for their contract stipulated that a first payment was to be made on touching Byzantine territory; four ounces of gold a month for the armoured cavalry, two for the light horse, one for the foot soldier, and four months' pay in advance. But it was not only the pay that cheered them; there were friendly faces, fresh food and water and, one likes to believe, an issue of the sweet, strong wine that still carries Monemvasia's name, long since corrupted to Malmsey.

There was also a message from the Emperor Andronicus II, bidding them hurry, for time was precious. The co-emperor and son of Andronicus, Michael IX, had led an army against the Osmanli Turks who were threatening Byzantium's remaining possessions in Asia Minor. He was defeated in a pitched battle and fled, abandoning the important towns of Nicaea, Nicomedia and Broussa (Iznik, Izmit and Bursa).* At the second encounter, although still in command of superior forces, he declined to engage the enemy. Most of his troops were mercenaries, Alani or Massagetes from the south of Russia; a temperamental people, as we shall see, they turned on their Byzantine general, Alexios Raoul the Grand Domestic,[1] and killed him. We cannot say whether Michael intended fighting again when he had regrouped his forces on the Artaki (Erdek) peninsula; he was not lacking in personal bravery but he probably distrusted his troops' steadiness as much as they feared his leadership. It is therefore likely that he proposed returning to Constantinople, but before he could cross to Europe he fell suddenly ill at Cyzicus; his father sent him physicians and a potent remedy, the oil which had burned in the church lamps during the mass of intercession for his recovery. At the moment when the monk bearing the miracle drug embarked in Constantinople, Michael dreamed that a superbly clad lady removed a nail from the site of the malady. It is a fair inference that he was delirious and going through the crisis of lobar pneumonia, and that he was already convalescent when the oil arrived.

By now nine-tenths of Asia Minor had been lost and with pardonable exaggeration the emperor is described as looking out from his palace at Blachernae to watch the Turkish hordes brandishing their scimitars on the far side of the Bosphorus. Andronicus II, who was forty-four at this time, remains an enigma for historians. He was deeply religious, as religion was understood; Miller wrote of him, 'Nature had intended him for a professor of theology, to which

* Modern names will be given in brackets throughout.

8

engrossing subject he devoted what time he could spare from the neglect of his civil and military duties.' But the pedant had hidden depths: a man in whose veins flowed the blood of four imperial lines, Ducas, Comnenos, Angelos and Palaeologos, could not be so transparently simple. Between his all-night sessions with the Patriarch and his prolonged studies of the *filioque* clause that had split the Christian Church, he inaugurated civil and judicial reforms; that these failed was due as much to his spendthrift brother Constantine and his inefficient advisers as to his own lack of resolution. He also took time off to sire two children by his first wife, four by his second and an unknown number of bastards. One illegitimate daughter was offered as a matrimonial pledge to Ghazan, the Mongol khan of Persia.

In view of his deeds I cannot picture him as the absent-minded, unworldly, professorial figure of earlier authors. He was shrewd enough, on more than one occasion, to play his enemies off against each other and crafty enough to have engineered the massacre of 1305 and let his son take the blame. Perhaps his greatest subtlety lay in concealing his subtlety: *ars est celare artem*. His portraits do not help us to an assessment of his character or capabilities; in the series of eight adult emperors whose miniatures are in the Louvre, that of Andronicus II is distinguished by his white beard and the small, closely set eyes. But in fairness to him it must be added that no prudent stroller would care to meet any of them on a dark night.

It was still September[2] when the excited inhabitants of Constantinople heard that the relieving fleet was in sight, and they flocked to see it enter the Golden Horn and discharge its passengers at the Blachernae wharf. As the Spaniards filed past the enthroned emperor, a scene imaginatively portrayed by Moreno Carbonero, they must have scanned the resplendent ranks of courtiers and the noble buildings with an appreciative eye. Another soldier was to say, of a different capital, five hundred years later, 'What a city to loot!' They were not to know how poor was this last remnant of the Roman empire; that glass was used for jewellery, pewter for silver. Since the blight of the fourth Crusade had descended on Constantinople, nothing but misfortune had befallen the hapless city.

The Byzantine emperors, before perishing, squandered much of their wealth in bribes to the Crusaders. The latter had then captured the city, murdered, raped and looted for three days, melted down gold and silver altar furniture and loaded the bullion on their mules in the very churches. Systematic extortion of public and private wealth followed; holy relics, which at that time had an inflated cash value, so that they often figured in royal dowries or indemnities, were shipped away. Most of them went to Venice, but there was enough to spare for France and Burgundy. Hardly a church in the west could not boast a nail or a sliver of wood from the True Cross, or a few drops of the Blessed Virgin's milk. The head of St James the Lesser went to Halberstadt, that of St Stephen to Soissons, which also received one head of John the Baptist; another (he appears to have had two, apart from a lower jaw in Oviedo, Spain) went to Amiens. Under the combined stimuli of piety and greed the Crusaders overlooked very little; even a phial containing a specimen of the breath of the donkey that was present at the manger in Bethlehem found its way to Italy.[3]

Under the Latin emperors, who took over the eastern Roman empire, or more precisely all but the three-eighths that went to the Venetians, the city's degradation continued. When Baldwin II, the last of a feeble line, bowed to the inevitable and ran away, he took with him what he could lay his hands on; thus the first of the Palaeologos dynasty, making his triumphant return in 1261, found his capital in a sorry state. Even the lead had disappeared from the palace roof and was doing duty as coinage. We may the more easily picture the joy that greeted the safe arrival of the expensive Catalans and Aragonese, for they represented the last throw of a ruined gambler. Whatever we may think of their subsequent behaviour we must concede that their presence saved the empire and the Palaeologi, menaced by Turks, Bulgars, Venetians and the far more dangerous Angevins. Thanks to the Catalan Company, they would survive for another century and a half.

> These, in the day when heaven was falling,
> The hour when earth's foundations fled,
> Followed their mercenary calling
> And took their wages and are dead.
> (A. E. Housman, *Epitaph on an Army of Mercenaries*)

The Byzantines looked at their future deliverers with astonishment. The fame of the Almugavars had preceded them and the crowd expected to see their money's worth. Who knows how they had pictured their new allies? Some, no doubt, as the Grecian heroes of old, their own forefathers, in bronze cuirasses and helmets gleaming under horsehair crests. Others, more realistic, might expect warriors armed cap-à-pie, coats of mail, visored helmets and emblazoned shields. Different indeed were the hairy savages who filed past the Blachernae palace to their quarters outside the walls, where the Eyüp Mosque now stands and where Pierre Loti used to sit on summer evenings, ruminating on the historic city spread before him.

The origin of the name Almugavar (the stress is on the third syllable) is itself a mystery, like so much of their early history, and its Arabic look possibly fortuitous. They were light infantry, skirmishers, forerunners of the *voltigeurs* of the French Republican armies. But they could fight in formation too; only well-trained troops can change smoothly from open order to closed ranks in the heat of the battle, but the discipline of the Almugavars was equal to this, and many other tests.

> Born in battle, war their trade;
> Of coarsest skins their finery made;
> The hard ground for their bed of ease;
> Cradle and bier—a shield for these.*

A hauberk covered head and shoulders; for uniform they wore a tunic, a fur jacket, gaiters and leather sandals. Add unshorn hair, wild beards and women of comparable aspect, and you have an idea of their impact on the astonished Greeks. Says one Spanish author:[4] 'Of excellent stature, very powerful, well proportioned, spare and agile, inured to toil and fatigue, rapid in march, firm in fight, reckless of life, eager for close combat, their warlike ferocity eclipsed that of the Greek and Roman legionaries.'

Their arms were, it seems, their only clean possessions, sharp and bright at all times; a spear, two javelins[5] and the short, murderous Iberian sword that Scipio Africanus had adopted for the Roman legions. At a sudden alarm they would clash their weapons and above the clatter would be heard the terrifying '*Aur! Aur! Desperta ferre!*' ('Iron, awake!'), an invocation that recalls the magic of that new metal in the minds of Bronze Age men and the legends of Wayland the Smith. In Castile the Almugavars were organized into

---

*   *Nacidos en batalla, es la guerra*
Su profesión; sus galas, burdas pieles;
Su lecho de placer, la dura tierra;
Y su cuna y sepulcro, los broqueles
(J. Xandri Pich, *Espa~a Legendaria*, Madrid, Yagües, 1934, p. 71.)

grades, with corresponding pay and status. The *sencillo*, or private, carried his own bread and found water and herbs to go with it; the *Almocadén* (Arabic—*Al-mokkadem*) carried a lance and pennant; of higher rank was the mounted Almugavar, and the commanding officer had another Arabic title, *Adalid*. The mounted troops of the expedition wore protective armour, chain or lizard mail, a helmet and various pieces of plate metal such as greaves and a cuirass, according to taste and means. An armoured horseman of this period appears in a fresco in the Chapel of St Agatha (Agueda), in the old city of Barcelona.

The Catalan Company was first recruited as an expeditionary force in 1281 by Peter III ('the Great') of Aragon on his way to conquests in North Africa and, later, Sicily. In its ranks were men from every part of Spain, including Christians and even Arabs from the Moorish kingdom of Granada; the great majority were Catalans (even the Aragonese accounted for less than five per cent) and the language of the Company and its successors remained the Catalan variety of the Langue d'Oc. In the ranks were many *Golfines*, more properly *Delfines* (French—*dauphins*), younger sons with no prospects beyond what their swords could win them.[6]

Nothing that I have written can convey an idea of the desperate courage and ferocity of these men—and women. In one of the combined operations that were so frequent during the Sicilian war, the departing fleet saw that an Almugavar had been left behind and that five mounted men-at-arms were making towards him. His officer, another Almugavar, prayed the admiral to put him back on shore, but he arrived too late, for his man had been killed when he landed. Desclot describes how he attacked the first horseman with a javelin throw that pierced his coat of mail and drove through the centre of his breast and so killed him. Leaping aside, he met the next assailant, thrusting his lance through the horse, which fell dead on its rider, so that he could no longer rise. The three remaining Frenchmen, astounded and enraged, now charged him. At the first he cast his remaining javelin, through helmet and skull into the brain, so that he too fell dead. The other two were carried past by their impetus, giving the Almugavar time to go back to the rider pinned under his dead horse and cut his throat. The two survivors now rode to get between him and the sea, whereupon he hurled a stone at the first, with such good aim that he hit him in the mouth and broke his jaw, at which the Frenchman turned his horse and made off. The Almugavar thrust his lance at the last attacker, through hauberk and thigh, then withdrew it and speared the horse. As the shaft snapped the wounded Frenchman had time to get home a blow with his sword, making a wound of the size of a handsbreadth. Weak now from loss of blood and reduced to his sword alone, the Almugavar was wading out to sea when he was overtaken by another party of the enemy and killed. 'But dearly was he bought,' says the old chronicler.[7]

An episode that is more widely known (it was even quoted by the Italian historian Amari) concerns a party of Almugavars taken prisoner and brought before the Prince of the Morea, son of Charles of Anjou, King of Naples. He showed surprise at the ragged dress and unkempt appearance of the captives and, on being told that they were the fierce Almugavars, 'Certes,' he said, 'I know not what worth there may be in you, nor what address, for to me you seem caitiff, poor and savage.'

' 'Tis true,' answered one, 'that I am one of the humblest of us all, yet notwithstanding, an there be one of your knights, of the best you have, gladly would I fight with him. And let him be mounted and armed as he will, but give me my lance, my javelin and my sword. And if I win in this encounter, then I am to go free from here without let; but if he should prove the better man, then do with me what you will.'

And so it was agreed. The Almugavar was set alone in the field, with only the arms he had asked, and the knight, fully armed, galloped at him with couched lance. The Almugavar stood his ground until the last moment; then he hurled his javelin with such force that it sank two handsbreadths into the horse's breast, leaping aside to avoid the lance. Down came horse and rider, and in a flash the Almugavar was on the fallen knight, sawing away at his helmet thongs that he might more easily cut his throat. Hereupon the prince stopped the comedy and gave the Almugavar fair raiment and a safe passage home. The tale, you may be sure, lost nothing in the telling, and when it came to the ears of King Peter in Sicily he courteously released ten French knights; they took with them the promise that, for every Almugavar set free, ten French knights would be sent in exchange. Peter was a noted poet and musician; he now showed that he was proficient in psychological warfare too.[8]

The womenfolk were fairly matched with their men. Muntaner, the doughty warrior and kindly chronicler of the expedition, tells of a woman of Perellada who went outside the walls to collect cabbages. As the French besiegers were present in force she put on a tunic of mail, wore belt and sword and took spear and shield with her to the allotment. Almost before she could begin to collect the vegetables a French knight appeared at the fence. Without hesitation she hurled the spear with such force that it pierced his coat of mail, his thigh and saddle, and buried its point in the horse. Thereafter she had little difficulty in bringing him back to Perellada, where Mercadera (so called because she was a marketeer) was congratulated by royalty and eventually received the 200 gold florins of her prisoner's ransom.[9]

Such fighters would obey no ordinary leader and to follow their fortunes you should know something of Roger de Flor. His career is a romantic one and its origin goes back to the days of the Emperor Frederick Hohenstaufen (1197–1250). Frederick's mother was the last of the Norman rulers of Sicily; his father was Holy Roman Emperor. Their son—nicknamed *Stupor Mundi*, the Wonder of the World—was a man of the Renaissance born two centuries too soon; his hobby was falconry (he had many others, from women to algebra, irrelevant to this tale) and the illustrated book that he wrote on this subject for his son Manfred can still be admired. His chief falconer was the handsomest man of his time, the German Richard von Blum. For him Frederick arranged a good match, choosing a patrician maiden of Brindisi, Beatrice Novoli. On Frederick's death Manfred inherited the kingdom of Sicily but lost his life fighting against the usurper Charles of Anjou, who had been invited by the Pope to invade Southern Italy and wipe out the Hohenstaufens, his inveterate enemies. (See Appendix.)

Table 1

Some heirs of Frederick II Hohenstaufen

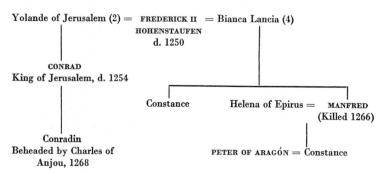

Richard von Blum, loyal to the House of Hohenstaufen, next went to help young Conradin, grandson of Frederick and last male claimant to the throne of Sicily. At Tagliacozzo Conradin was defeated and Richard killed. Charles of Anjou, one of the more vindictive kings, not only had Conradin executed publicly but seized the possessions of all his supporters. Beatrice thus found herself penniless in Palermo; a fishing boat took her and her two young sons to Brindisi, but once there she found no trace of her family. Wandering famished near the quay she fainted, as it chanced, at the door of a brothel. All the world knows that prostitutes have hearts of gold and Beatrice was taken in and cared for; the story (and it is only a story) goes on to relate that she was taken on the strength of the establishment and was thenceforth known as La Bruna.[10] Her son Rutger (history is silent regarding the fate of her elder son, James) ran wild; from childhood he haunted the harbour and one winter, when he was eight years old, he roused the interest of Vassaill, a French ship's captain. Master of one of the Templars' vessels, laid up for the usual winter cleaning and caulking, he took a liking to the lad and offered to teach him a sailor's trade. Beatrice gladly surrendered to Vassaill the care of her son; perhaps to mark the beginning of a new era, or possibly because his German name came haltingly to French and Italian tongues, he translated it from Rutger von Blum to Roger de Flor.

Roger's character has to be deduced from his actions rather than from the accounts of partisan historians. Physical bravery may be taken for granted, for no one could rise as he did without it. That he held himself in high esteem can also be inferred: his negotiations with the Emperor of Byzantium were conducted with a self-confidence amounting almost to arrogance. 'These are my terms . . . The title of Grand Duke . . . a royal bride . . .'; a man who knew his own worth and the other's need. His parentage ensured that Latin bravado was backed by Teutonic pertinacity; that flamboyant postures concealed shrewd motives. Intelligent and ambitious, truculent when courtesy had shot its bolt, one sometimes became aware, too late, that he was a man to fear.

Little is known of his personal appearance, other than the vague description of Pachymeres, quoted later. It is a fair assumption that he was well built, for even as a child he is said to have scampered up and round the Templars' rigging like a monkey, and as a grown man he was a noted warrior. If heredity played a part he was handsome and by the same token he had an even chance of being light haired

15

and above the average height. The rolling walk of the sailor, the arrogant tilt of the head and the cocked, bearded chin are my own inferences, but they paint a plausible portrait of the brilliant and unscrupulous adventurer.

For some years Roger sailed with Vassaill, learning the duties of a sailor and mastering the art of navigation. So well did he progress that he was known as a first-class seaman by the time he was twenty. We find scattered references to how he spent the next six years. Fighting the corsairs of Barbary was merely a part of Mediterranean seafaring, but Roger was as efficient in this as in other branches of his trade. He was promoted to the command of a new vessel, the *Falcon* (happy omen for the son of Richard von Blum!) and was made a serving- or sergeant-brother of the Temple. And it is as Brother Roger that Muntaner refers to this adventurer until his arrival at Constantinople with the Catalan Company. He learned to speak Greek fluently and either married or forgot to marry a Cypriot lady, by whom he had a daughter.

On 18 May 1291, when he was twenty-six, he enters the pages of history books. The Mamelukes under Melek Ashraf Kelaun were besieging Acre and Templars made up the greater part of the garrison of this, the last fortified port of the Crusaders in Syria. Roger fought alongside the doomed defenders so well that he is credited with killing a Saracen leader. But the walls were breached, the defenders outnumbered. For the men there remained only death in battle; for the rest the slave market. The quay was thronged with desperate women, willing to pay any price for a passage to safety, while the sounds of slaughter, rape and pillage crept inexorably nearer to the harbour.

Brother Roger fought for as long as there seemed some hope of holding off the enemy. When this vanished he prudently returned to his or rather the Temple's ship, and prepared to save whom he could from the disaster—but only the wealthy and especially those whose wealth was in portable form. By the time the haggling was over and his galley rowed out of the harbour of Acre, leaving helpless, despairing Christians to the ravening Mamelukes, Roger was a rich man. It is impossible to say whether he also helped himself to the Templars' funds, as has been alleged; the jewels of the damsels in distress would by themselves amount to a tidy sum. The now penniless ladies were put ashore in Cyprus and Roger sailed on to Marseilles, his home port.

16

It was not long before ugly rumours caught up with him and reached the ears of the Grand Master of the Temple. Added to the story of his behaviour at Acre was the accusation of having sold fellow Christians to the Saracens on other occasions. The arrival of a French lady, one of his passengers from Acre, brought matters to a head: Roger's expulsion from the Temple was decreed and he was denounced to Pope Boniface VIII as a thief and apostate. We may be sure that his Hohenstaufen connection would make him unpopular in that quarter. Roger was described by the contemporary Greek chronicler, George Pachymeres, as 'a man in the prime of life, of terrible aspect, quick in gesture and impetuous in all his actions.' His wits were sharp too and he left Marseilles in time to escape the hue and cry. Genoa was his destination, for, although he had to leave the *Falcon* in Marseilles, he had enough friends in Italy to ensure his future. Ticino Doria, one of the early members of the great Doria family, helped him to buy a galley, the *Olivetta*, and collect a crew with whom he sailed against the Saracens. This at least was the ostensible and praiseworthy object of the venture; in fact he was not particular whom he attacked, if his prey showed any evidence of wealth. One by one he captured vessels and increased his fleet, finding crews eager enough to serve such a fortunate captain, on such lucrative business.

He is said to have given up piracy and tendered his fleet to the Angevins; an unlikely story; they were allies of a Pope who wanted nothing better than to have the thief and apostate in his power. According to the story, the offer was refused and Roger went on to pillage the coasts of Spain, France, Italy and North Africa indiscriminately. Immensely wealthy, he next offered his services to Frederick, King of Sicily, and was appointed admiral in the war against the Angevins.[11] Now for the first time he commanded Almugavars; mutual respect was established, for the wild soldiers were quick to appreciate a man who could fight as fiercely as they did and was even more predatory, if that were possible.

When peace was signed at Caltabellotta in Sicily, the Catalan Company had to look for employment elsewhere. Roger was strongly attracted to the east, if only because he would be out of reach of Pope and Templars; the danger from the former was especially threatening, since peace had been made and Frederick of Sicily might presumably be persuaded to hand him over to the Pope. He accordingly sent two envoys to Andronicus ('Would that

Table 2

Some essential relationships between the Byzantine imperial families, the Kingdom of Bulgaria and Roger de Flor

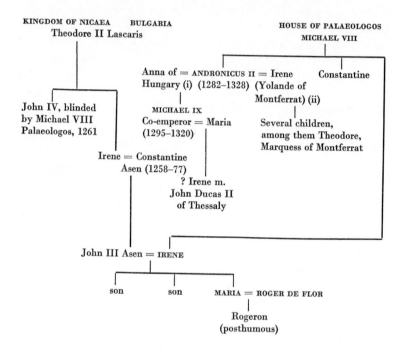

KINGDOM OF NICAEA   BULGARIA   HOUSE OF PALAEOLOGOS
Theodore II Lascaris   MICHAEL VIII

Anna of = ANDRONICUS II = Irene   Constantine
Hungary (i) (1282–1328) (Yolande of

John IV, blinded   MICHAEL IX   Montferrat) (ii)
by Michael VIII   Co-emperor = Maria
Palaeologos, 1261   (1295–1320)   Several children,
among them Theodore,
Marquess of Montferrat

Irene = Constantine
Asen (1258–77)
? Irene m.
John Ducas II
of Thessaly

John III Asen = IRENE

son   son   MARIA = ROGER DE FLOR

Rogeron
(posthumous)

it had never happened,' says Pachymeres), offering his services and those of the Almugavars for nine months, at double the usual rates of pay. For himself—and his demands show how far the urchin of Brindisi had progressed—he asked the following: first, the title of μέγας κύριος, or Great Lord, usually referred to by westerners as Magaduque or Grand Duke. In the latter form it survived in Russia long after the fall of Byzantium. It was equivalent to commander-in-chief of all armed forces; at that time it ranked fifth in the Byzantine hierarchy, in which there were at least eighty-two grades, continually changing in precedence. His second condition was that he receive in marriage the hand of the emperor's niece, Maria (see Table 2). Third, for his chief of staff, Corberán d'Alet, the title of Seneschal of the Empire.

The embassy returned promptly with a favourable answer to all requests, a letter of appointment written with cinnabar and sealed with gold, a handsome document, and various badges of office: there was a ceremonial lance and pennant for Roger, and the towering bonnet appropriate to his new rank, for headgear took the place of our badges and, in the case of the more senior officers, was decorated with pearls and gold braid, almost literally a 'brass hat'. King Frederick of Sicily was only too pleased to congratulate Roger on his new dignity; the Almugavars had by now become an embarrassment, unruly and expensive. Their belief that they had a right to anyone's property, be he friend or enemy, caused complications and on all counts Frederick was relieved when their departure had been decided.

With the Almugavars went 1,500 horsemen and 1,000 infantry of the conventional kind. They travelled in thirty-nine transports and galleys, whose crews were equally renowned as fighters. As he could no longer afford to employ them, the costs of the journey were partly met by Frederick; their commander, Roger de Flor, paid the rest from his own pocket, helped by a loan of 20,000 ducats from Genoese merchants. Apart from this, Frederick gave each man a bonus of a hundredweight of biscuit, two pounds of cheese, garlic, onions, and a carcass of salt pork to every four. Of course there were grumblers who thought their services were poorly rewarded with a bag of provender, but the general mood was one of elation. They looked back without regret at the plume of smoke on Etna, the shore line of Sicily and the Calabrian peaks; and their hearts were high as they gazed over the deep blue sea ahead and thought of stern fighting against new enemies and of the boundless wealth of the east.

Chapter 2

First blood
1302–3

Delighted though they were at the arrival of the Catalan mercenaries, we may be sure that the emperors' reception of their leaders was conducted according to the rules. There would be dead silence, as always in the august presence; the visitor would be conducted to the throne and supported by two attendants, as though the sight of such majesty had loosened his limbs; and the customary incense would be burned at the ceremony of Roger's promotion to patrician rank. It is doubtful whether ritual prostration was insisted on, for it was regarded more as a privilege than a sign of subservience. It was therefore accorded to the mayor of the Genoese colony, but the representatives of the Venetians and Franks were excluded from the προσκύνησις or *adoratio*. Each leader, however, had to sink on one knee when forty paces from the throne and presents or insignia that were graciously conferred had to be accepted with the hands shielded in a fold of the recipient's robe, for a universal taboo holds that direct contact with majesty is positively dangerous (see note 1 to Prologue).

We can only imagine the effect of such ceremony on Roger's companions, rude soldiers for the most part, especially when the audience was terminated by the emperor's Ἄπελθε, ποίησον μίνσας, a simple paraphrase of the *Ite, missa est* with which the Latin Mass is concluded. And the wedding! Never had they seen such magnificence. Choirs sang ritual hymns that were unchanged since the days of Justinian; silks and furs provided a background of splendour

20

to the gold and jewels of collars, belts and pendant earrings. Precedence for each grade was rigidly defined and jealously guarded, so that even the celebrated Varangian bodyguard carried their axes in the second row behind the emperor.

The bride received a good press from eye-witnesses. She was sixteen, beautiful and intelligent; her looks would be predictable, for imperial dynasties had for centuries anticipated natural selection by choosing brides in the same way as modern beauty queens. If tradition was followed and Roger saw her for the first time when she raised her veil on the wedding morning, he would be well pleased. To the Spanish troops and their womenfolk the sight of Christian ladies in *yashmaks* must have seemed strange; they were not to know that the Moslems of Spain, among whom they had no doubt noted the custom, derived it originally from Byzantium. The state banquet that followed was organized on routine lines down to the final kick of the last dancer and the gold saucer before each guest was pressed upon him as a present when he left, an age-old custom. Now, however, there was a modification, for a servant nonchalantly took it back at the door, so that both ceremonial and Treasury were appeased.

The Genoese looked on the arrival of the Catalan Company with misgivings. They had always found rival Catalan merchants to be as astute, brave and enterprising as they themselves and they feared that Roger's arrival might have commercial as well as military significance. They therefore tried to make use of a curious and somewhat involved set of circumstances. Charles of Valois, politically independent of the grasping Angevins, was another Frenchman with an acquisitive eye on Constantinople; he had married Catherine de Courtenay, heiress to the Latin dynasty which had fled so ignominiously in 1261, and was therefore regarded as the logical claimant to her inheritance. He was also regarded as something of a joke, an almost professional pretender to various thrones; the Catalans christened him *'rei del xapeu e del vent'*, for his politics were as erratic as a hat snatched off by the wind.[1] Charles had approached Frederick of Sicily (the Almugavars' former employer) and obtained from him a promise to support an expedition against the Byzantine empire. Andronicus knew well enough that it had diplomatic value only and that he had nothing to fear from the king of Sicily. The Genoese insinuation, that Roger had arrived to implement the agreement made with Charles of Valois, therefore made

him smile in his beard; behind his hand of course. The Genoese had
allowed success to go to their heads and the Emperor was not sorry
that they should feel alarmed; though outwardly all was harmony,
the Greeks resented the obvious prosperity of the Genoese while
their own empire was becoming poorer and less secure.

Roger's wedding had been a splendid affair. Late that night, when
the last guest had left, a sudden commotion in the Blachernae quarter roused the citizens. As usual, Greek and Spanish writers dis-
agree about the cause. The former maintain that the Genoese had
demanded, and been refused payment of, the 20,000 ducats advanced to Roger in Sicily; the story carries the improbability of a
moneylender disturbing the bridal night of a princess. The Spanish
relate how an Almugavar, wandering on a sightseeing tour, was
annoyed by two Genoese making fun of his uncouth appearance.
Unversed in the niceties of debate, the Almugavar drew his sword
and ran it through one of the Genoese. Partisans of both sides
appeared and quickly continued the argument. The brawl became
a riot, the riot a battle. A Genoese officer, Roseo del Final, un-
wisely put the dispute on an international level by bringing out the
Genoese banner and began attacking isolated parties of Almugavars,
whose billets were scattered throughout the quarter. The Company's cavalry now appeared, the Almugavars had time to form their
ranks and the streets of Constantinople heard the dreaded '*Desperta
ferre!*' as the Catalans launched themselves on their opponents.
Roseo del Final was soon killed and his banner trodden underfoot.

Andronicus, who had watched the brawl with satisfaction, now
thought the fighting had gone far enough to teach the Genoese a
lesson; though he could contemplate a few hundred of their corpses
with equanimity, he knew that a massacre of the whole colony would
be prejudicial to the state. For one thing, Byzantium was now too
poor to afford a navy and relied on Genoa for defence at sea. He
therefore sent one of his senior naval officers, Stephen Marzala, to
quell the riot, only to see him cut down and torn to pieces. The
Almugavars were by now as single-minded as a pack of hounds on
a breast-high scent; they had unfurled their banners and were resolved to attack and sack Pera, cutting the throats of all whom they
encountered. Only the voice of the huntsman could stop them now;
Andronicus himself went to the nuptial chamber and begged Roger
to call off his men. This he did promptly enough, but not before
3,000 Genoese lay dead in the streets. Note that here and throughout

this narrative the number of enemy wounded is not given: no enemy wounded survived. Andronicus is said to have been so impressed with the Company's obedience to its own leader that he ordered another four months' pay, a story that takes some believing. Roger returned to his bride.

So far only the Genoese had suffered. Nevertheless the Greeks would feel safer with their formidable allies at a distance; Andronicus felt too that it was time his expensive gamble began to pay off and suggested that the new Grand Duke, no longer Brother Roger in Muntaner's chronicle, should take his men across the Sea of Marmara to fight the Turks. Having chased co-Emperor Michael out of Asia, they were now besieging the town of Cyzicus and the peninsula of Artaki (Erdek) on which it stood. The narrow neck was defended by a strong wall that was ceaselessly assaulted by the Turks. Twelve thousand cavalry and 100,000 infantry employed by Byzantium had not dared to challenge this same force of Turks in the open field. Now the Emperor wanted to launch 1,500 horse and 4,000 foot against them. Even allowing for the exaggerated numbers of the Byzantine force—intended to emphasize the achievements of the Spaniards—it would be a crucial test of the tactics and fighting qualities of the Catalans.

Before agreeing to move Roger made a further condition. He insisted on the appointment of Ferdinand d'Aonés, one of his officers of noble birth, as admiral of the combined operation; he also demanded—and how these disguised commands must have irritated the Greeks—that Aonés be given a royal bride as a further guarantee against treachery. It was thus that the prudent Grand Duke ensured that his naval support would be in trustworthy hands and that the hostile Genoese would be kept away from his line of communications and possible retreat. It is as well to emphasize Roger's caution, in the light of future events.

The Catalan Company was reinforced by a picked detachment of Greeks under Marulles, a Byzantine nobleman, and the Alani mercenaries, led by their chief, George, also referred to as Gircon, possibly another version of the same name. The Alani were presumably those who had mutinied and killed Raoul, their general. There were 16,000 of them, but only half were fighting men for, like most contemporary mercenaries, they travelled with their women and children.[2] Thus Roger's army was larger than one would gather from Spanish sources, even if not homogeneous in quality.

The wall of the Artaki peninsula was under attack every day from morning to sunset, and the day of Roger's arrival was no exception. When darkness came the Turks retired to their camp to sleep, without posting sentinels, so little respect had they for the aggressive qualities of the Byzantines. Meanwhile Roger had quietly disembarked his army on the peninsula, out of sight of the besiegers. His scouts told him that the Turkish camp was about two leagues away, on a plateau between two gullies. When the troops paraded, the cavalry bore the imperial standard and that of the new Grand Duke, but the Almugavars hoisted the colours of the King of Aragón[3] and those of his brother Frederick, King of Sicily. Throughout the story which unfolds the ruffians remained faithful to the sovereigns who were so eager to be rid of them. The pales of Aragon went with them, from the Taurus mountains to Athens, the regular herald of victory and always carried with sublime confidence at the head of the column instead of in the centre, where it could best be defended. Corberán d'Alet, seneschal of the army, rode in front of the Almugavars, a valiant young leader who had Roger's confidence and affection.[4] The Grand Duke himself rode with Marulles in the van of the cavalry.

At midnight they crossed the wall that defended the isthmus and at first light launched themselves at the camp of the sleeping Turks. Men, women and children woke to the clash of steel, the cries of the dying and the sinister '*Aur! Aur! Desperta ferre!*', to many the last sound they would hear on earth. Without time to form their ranks and hemmed in by the flanking gullies, they fought to the death in isolated groups, the sight of their butchered families adding to their desperation. Many tried to rescue their women and children and were overtaken in their hampered flight. When full daylight came 3,000 Turkish horsemen and ten thousand infantry lay dead on the blood-soaked plateau and no male above the age of ten remained alive. The captive women and children were put on board the galleys and sent as presents to the empresses and to Roger's bride, and every man contributed from his booty to the present they sent to Roger's mother-in-law, the Princess Irene.

Great was the joy of the troops and greater still that of the Byzantine court when the tokens of victory arrived only a week after the departure of the Catalan Company.[5] But the Genoese took the news sullenly and without comment. Co-emperor Michael, too, was resentful when he heard how rapidly such a small force had routed the Turks; he remembered his own defeat and his craven retreat when his own troops had actually outnumbered the same enemy. His malice was to cost the Company dear. The most profound effect, however, was not on their employers, but on their enemies the Ottoman Turks. Even Nikephoros Gregoras, a contemporary and hostile Byzantine writer, gives the Company credit for the precipitate retreat of the Ottomans, who would not again trouble Byzantium for some years.

It was October and the country before them unknown; it was too late in the year to undertake an organized pursuit and Roger ordered his troops back to Artaki the same night. On 1 November the weather changed suddenly: icy winds blew from the Anatolian plateau and the Russian steppes, and torrents of rain turned roads into streams and streams into roaring rivers. Winter is no time for campaigning in Asia Minor and billets were requisitioned on the peninsula. The Grand Duke sent for his wife and her family, asking them to exchange the luxury of the palace for the winter quarters of a campaigner; the fleet, under Aonés, sailed to Chios, where country and climate were delightful and little notice was taken of its tenancy by the Genoese merchant prince, Benedict Zaccaria.

The troops were billeted under rigid rules: six representatives of the army formed a council with an equal number of the Greek inhabitants in order to fix the price of victuals, to be paid for out of the soldiers' wages at the end of March. It is sad to relate that the Catalans had not changed since leaving Sicily. Apart from victualling, the Greeks were treated as conquered enemies, instead of liberated allies; their goods and their womenfolk alike were regarded as the troops' perquisites and Roger closed his eyes to their barbarous behaviour. But one of his senior and more aristocratic officers, Ferdinand Jiménez d'Arenós, resigned from the Company in disgust and took service with Guy de la Roche, Duke of Athens. We are not told whether it was the normal behaviour of the Almugavars or some specific incident that prompted Jiménez to take his troops away from what promised to be such a profitable venture. Some authors ignore the event; Moncada hints that Roger interfered with the handling of Jiménez's men; others believe that Jiménez could not acquiesce with such evident lack of discipline. The whole question of the Company's behaviour is one for which no final answer can be given. Muntaner is regarded as the most reliable chronicler of these events, and has nothing to say regarding the winter at Artaki. The

Greeks, on the other hand, have a smaller reputation for factual reporting; none of their chroniclers was an eyewitness of the Anatolian campaigns, as was Muntaner. The truth probably lies somewhere between the extremes: the times were rough, free companies were notoriously destructive and the behaviour of the Catalans neither angelic nor diabolic.

Here I may quote the first Byzantine account of the Catalan Company's excesses, serving as a model for all subsequent descriptions. With very few details added or subtracted it was used as a formula for the behaviour of the Spaniards in the years that followed, suggesting a singular lack of originality on the part of the Catalans—or the authors. Says Gregoras,[6]

> It was dreadful to see the goods of the unfortunate Romans
> snatched away, girls and women violated, old men and priests
> carried off into captivity, victims of the punishments, ever new,
> to which the impious hands of the Latins subjected them; and
> seeing the sword poised continually over their necks, to kill
> them if they did not reveal their treasures and wealth. Those
> who gave up everything were reduced to beggary; those who
> had not the means to buy their freedom had their hands or
> feet cut off and were exposed in the streets as a lamentable
> spectacle, that they might beg an obol or a crust, without other
> means of support than their tongues or their flowing tears.

Compared with the barbarous punishments that were regularly meted out by Byzantine justice the foregoing are comparatively mild. I mention this, not to excuse the Catalans but to point out the hypocrisy of the horror tales of Byzantine chroniclers.[7]

There is no doubt that tension was building up between the various races in the Artaki peninsula, and during the winter we learn that Michael punished the inhabitants of nearby Pegües for opening their gates to the Almugavars. Taking the larger view, it is apparent that the causes of enmity were more deeply rooted than contemporary writers indicated, or possibly knew. The split between Orthodox and Catholic, a slow fire that was sometimes damped down but always broke out afresh, aroused more passion than could the most atrocious deeds. Even writers of the nineteenth century drift into the use of terms such as 'impious Latins' and 'schismatic Greeks'. The Byzantines could not forget the boorish, destructive Crusaders; the Latins that their papal legate was murdered, their sick butchered in hospital and many of them sold into slavery by the Greeks, fellow Christians. And even while the friendless city was in its last agony, about to fall to the Turks, Luke Notaras the Grand Admiral said that he would rather see the Turkish turban in Constantinople than the cardinal's hat of the Latins.

March was blowing itself out, spring was near and Roger left for Constantinople with four galleys; he took with him his wife, her mother and her two brothers, all of whom had spent the winter at Cyzicus. Andronicus greeted him cordially; gold was handed over for a double instalment of the Company's pay and a farewell banquet arranged. Such generosity was almost beyond the meagre resources of the state and the court was now openly divided into factions. On one side was co-Emperor Michael, in turn impulsive and apprehensive, glowering and smarting under comparisons between his showing in the field and Roger's. The Patriarch supported him on religious, others on financial grounds and the Genoese neglected no chance of promoting dislike of the hated Catalans. Michael, it is said, was so disgusted at the treatment of his fellow-Greeks at Cyzicus that he refused Roger's routine request for an audience. His indignation accords not at all with the misery and virtual serfdom to which the Palaeologi had reduced their Greek subjects.

But Irene and her daughter were powerful advocates; it says much for his charm that Roger was so highly esteemed by two aristocrats brought up in the formal and exclusive atmosphere of the Byzantine court. An alternative explanation of their support will be reviewed later. The women would naturally remind Andronicus that the Almugavars, when they were in Constantinople, had shared their food with refugees from the Turkish hordes, when no help was forthcoming from their own kin. There may have been some substance in the plea; discrepancies among chroniclers do not help us to the truth, for history in those days did not even pretend to strive for impartiality. The old Emperor (Andronicus is always referred to as the Elder, to distinguish him from the grandson who later deposed him) issued only one command before the Grand Duke returned to Cyzicus: the city of Philadelphia must be relieved of its Turkish besiegers.

When Roger returned to Cyzicus he busied himself with the mundane tasks of preparing his army for the march as soon as the campaigning season should begin. His quartermasters reported, with long faces, that the Almugavars had run up victualling accounts amounting to eight or even ten months' pay, in the space of only four months. A curious and apparently accurate piece of history, which makes us wonder why these wild and wicked men had not simply helped themselves, as they were so consistently accused of doing. We are also entitled to suspect that the accounts were somewhat inflated; the Catalans would surely be no match for the wily Greeks when it came to accountancy.[8]

The trouble was quickly settled. At a public ceremony Roger paid over, from his own pocket, the total amount owed by his men and had the accounts thrown on a bonfire. The Almugavars thronged to kiss his hand, foreigner though he was; henceforth there was no task too difficult for them, if he commanded it. The reluctant tribute of Pachymeres, in its seventeenth-century French translation, effectively brings the adventurer into sharper focus: 'Il avoit une ardeur incroiable, et une adresse merveilleuse à gouverner la multitude des voleurs qu'il commandoit.' Never had his popularity reached such heights.

On 9 April, the day chosen for the start of the campaign of 1303, a dispute begween Alani and Almugavars broke out; the immediate cause was an indecent assault on a woman by one of the latter, in a flour-mill which was used by both parties. In a moment Cyzicus was in an uproar. Fighting became general and lasted all day; while the Alani barricaded themselves in their lodgings and hurled down tiles on the attackers, the Almugavars battered down doors and forced their opponents to withdraw, leaving hundreds of their dead behind. Among these was the son of Gircon, their leader. Roger appreciated the gravity of the occurrence and tried in vain to appease Gircon with blood money; blood, he was told, must be repaid with blood, not with gold. The offer itself was an insult and only a thousand of the Alani would now consent to remain under the command of the Grand Duke.

Chapter 3

Triumphs in Asia Minor
1303

The date of the march from Cyzicus is disputed, but we know that in early spring 6,000 Catalans, 1,000 Alani and a small contingent of Greeks under Marulles set off to the south. Their way led them up the fertile valley of the River Macestus (Simay) and their first task was to take Germes (Soma), a fortress on a crag in the shade of a mountain massif. They had traversed one of the richest agricultural regions of Anatolia, where since the days of classical Greece wheat and olives and vines had grown in profusion. The hills were as they are today, arid and stony, but pine forests and thickets of scrub oak and laurel relieve the bareness of the slopes and incidentally provide cover for enemies. The move against Germes was therefore precautionary, for it was a little to the west of the main road to Philadelphia (Alaşehir), and yet near enough to it for a Turkish garrison to menace their rear.

Luckily the fame of the Almugavars had preceded them and they came upon a retiring detachment instead of a defended fort. The first action of the campaign was thus fought by the vanguard, a minor success but a heartening one. For the news from Philadelphia was worse and desperate appeals arrived daily as the city's resources dwindled. In Constantinople Andronicus spent days and nights praying with the Patriarch. Roger, more practical, moved on by forced marches through Nakrasa (Maltepe, north of Kirkagaç), Thyatira (Akhisar), past Lake Coloe and across the River Hermos (Gediz). The route is hilly, not mountainous, but the distances

29

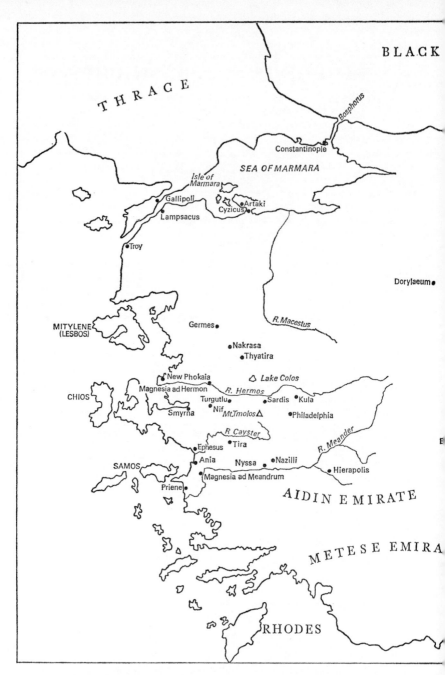

Map 1   Asia Minor, showing the extent of the Company's
journeyings from Cyzicus to the Iron Gates

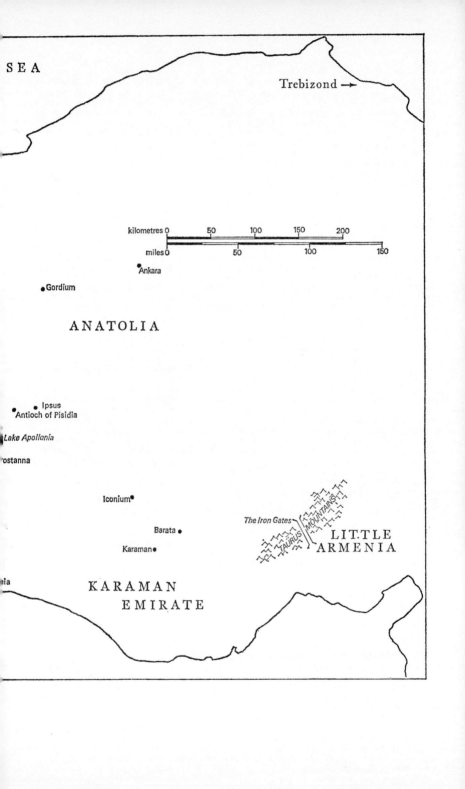

SEA

Trebizond →

kilometres 0   50   100   150   200
miles 0   50   100   150

• Ankara

• Gordium

ANATOLIA

• Ipsus
• Antioch of Pisidia

Lake Apollonia

ostanna

Iconium •

Barata •

Karaman •

The Iron Gates

TAURUS MOUNTAINS

LITTLE ARMENIA

ia

KARAMAN
EMIRATE

covered were great enough to impress Byzantine writers. Spanish troops have always been noted for their endurance and as late as the last century, the Carlist General Gómez marched his men eighty miles in twenty-four hours—in rope-soled sandals. To make the feat more remarkable the Almugavars were accompanied by their wives and children, who somehow maintained the pace of their men. On that weary road they sighted the barrows of the Lydian necropolis of Sardis, they passed by the ruins of the city of Croesus itself,[1] today the village of Sart; then they skirted the shoulder of the mountain that loomed over them, its sides riven into fantastic gorges, and debouched into the open plain.

And so they came to Philadelphia on their sandalled feet, after 120 miles of forced marches, ready for battle next day. They would scarcely have spared a glance, as they trudged along, for three of the seven churches of the Apocalypse—Thyatira, Sardis and Philadelphia itself. Nor would they care that the lands through which they had come had seen empires rise and fall before Constantinople or Barcelona built their first walls. The soldier, said Walter Bagehot, is not a romantic animal; they had come to make history, not to gaze at where it had been made before.

Philadelphia is today a sleepy town of a few thousand inhabitants, in a valley on the slope of Mount Tmolos (Boz Dagi). When the Catalans saw it they were looking at 'a noble city, one of the great ones of the world, all of eighteen miles around, as great a circumference as Rome or Constantinople'. Muntaner's enthusiastic appraisal of the city's size is probably exaggerated.[2] It is true that it stood at the head of an extremely fertile valley and that it was an important pilgrimage centre, but the only guide we have today is the north wall of the Byzantine town. This measures less than three-quarters of a mile and is difficult to reconcile with the estimate of the whole perimeter. The besiegers were Karamanli Turks, the most important of the Turkoman tribes and at that time far more powerful than the Osmanlis. They numbered 8,000 horse and 12,000 foot and were commanded by the emir Ali-Shîr of Karaman. If they were superior to the Grand Duke's force in numbers, they were inferior in discipline, tactics and arms; but they were just as eager as the Almugavars for the fighting to begin.

Roger divided his cavalry into three squadrons, Alani, Greeks and Spaniards, and Corberán de Alet likewise divided the infantry into three formations. The attack began at daybreak and as ever the

Company went forward with supreme resolution, crying *'Aragó!'* and *'Sant Jordi!'*, the first for the King of Catalonia and Aragón to whom they were still attached by sentiment, the second for their patron St George (today the city of Barcelona still quarters the red cross of St George with the pales of Aragón). The Turkish arrows, shot from a small, light bow, did little damage in the short time it took the opposing ranks to meet; the speed of the Company's advance was, in fact, one of their most effective tactical methods, as it reduced the time during which the advancing troops were exposed to missiles. On the plain near the aqueduct of Philadelphia, at Aulaca, the armies clashed, horse against horse, foot against foot.

The Turks fought bravely enough, but not with that combination of recklessness and discipline that distinguished the Catalan Company. The battle raged from sun-up till the hour of nones,[3] says the chronicler. The immense slaughter made by mail-clad horsemen among the lightly armed Turks, and the onslaught of the agile, ferocious Almugavars could not be endured for longer; only a thousand mounted Turks, including the wounded Ali-Shîr, and 500 infantry could save themselves by flight. Of Roger's men only 180 were killed. Ordering his troops to form their squadrons and battalions again, he followed the enemy cautiously in case of an ambush or a rally and then made a circuit of the walls of Philadelphia. (Incidentally, if the circumference had really been eighteen miles he would hardly have got his troops to cover the distance after a morning's hard fighting.) His caution was rewarded by seeing that the enemy's main force had disappeared and that even the garrisons of the besiegers' forts were melting away after their defeated comrades.

A sidelight on the unreliability of patriotic historians is afforded by Gregoras' version of the same event, the relief of Philadelphia, in which he ignores the battle completely:[4]

but when the Turks saw the military discipline, the gleam of their weapons and the superlative *élan* of the Latins, they fled, overcome by terror, not only far from the city, but beyond the ancient limits of the Roman empire. Such was that army, so well instructed in the use of their arms, so powerful in its numbers (since there campaigned with the Latins the pick of the Romans and all the army of the Alani[5]), that the enemy were beaten by their presence without daring to attempt anything. So much so that many say, that if the Emperor, fearful of other dangers, had not forbidden their advance, all the cities and Roman provinces would have been restored to his empire in a short time, free and cleansed of the enemy.

The magistrates and a great throng of citizens came out to welcome the victors, headed by the saintly Bishop Theoleptos, 'whose prayers', says Moncada, 'did more to defend the city than the arms of the garrison'. The entry was modelled on the Roman triumph; successful generals often cast their eyes back to the Romans when the idea of seizing power first occurs to them. Charlemagne, Rienzi and Napoleon readily come to mind. First came the cavalry, carrying the captured standards, the horse-tail banners of the vanquished Turks. Then followed carts heaped with spoils, a throng of captured women and children, and even a few youths spared from the customary massacre of all grown males. Last came the infantry, in their centre the officers of higher rank, mounted and displaying their standards.

Such a triumph had never been seen in Asia; to make it more impressive every Almugavar was dressed in brightly coloured silks or satin, found in the Turkish camp but of course originally taken from the Greeks. They did not concern themselves with the niceties of legal possession; the nine points were on their side. In this way may have arisen some of the accusations of plundering their allies in Philadelphia. Greek historians complain of the exorbitant war contributions later levied here by Roger; understandably Spanish authors do not refer to them. They tell us that two weeks were passed in feasting and every kind of entertainment that a grateful city could devise. A curious and significant note is struck in the remark by Moncada that gratitude is always forthcoming when people are in dire straits, but that it ceases once the peril is past. A truism that shows how conscious he was of the Greeks' resentment and the accusations of their chroniclers.

Roger had now completed his assignment. The campaigning season was not yet over, however, and the Company had come to fight and, of course, to loot. A choice presented itself: to follow the defeated Turks to their capital at Karaman, or to turn west and liberate the cities in the ancient territory of Ionia that were still in danger. There were sound reasons for making the second choice, for although the west coast of Anatolia had been made safe by Aonés and the fleet—the Greeks accused him of plundering Samos and

Mitylene as well as his base of Chios—the fertile inland valleys still harboured parties of marauding Turks. Once more the sober element in Roger's nature triumphed over the adventurous (I cannot emphasize this too often) and he decided to consolidate rather than to seek fresh laurels.

The first move was northward over the mountain, to take possession of the fortress of Kula, whence the Turkish garrison fled on hearing of his approach. Another enthusiastic welcome awaited him, the citizens allegedly making every effort to atone for having surrendered their city too readily to the Turks. Roger forgave them. For their leaders, however, he had little sympathy, as witness the affair of the Bulgarian Cranislaus, or Crisanislaus, so far as it can be reconstructed. Before being appointed governor by Andronicus he had spent several years in prison, in the time of Michael VIII. We know neither why he was shut up nor why he was set free. It is said that Roger reproached him openly for surrendering Kula, that the Bulgarian spoke strongly in his own defence and that Roger, who was daily becoming more autocratic, drew his sword, wounded him and then ordered his execution. After hanging for some time Cranislaus was found to be still alive; Greek officers took advantage of the miracle to urge that he be pardoned, if only to avoid the offence that the execution would give to the emperor.[6]

You may be sure that the event was soon known in Constantinople. It was whispered that the Grand Duke was dreaming of an independent kingdom in Asia Minor and, like a true soldier of fortune, had no scruples about hacking it out of the tottering empire of his employer. Among the accusations and rebuttals that still fly back and forth between patriotic scholars of the two nations, Roger's ambitions are given as the chief reason for the tragedy that was to unfold. In my opinion they are essential for a proper understanding of his fate. It must be confessed that, if he had the military genius of a Caesar or a Napoleon, their personal bravery and the gift of arousing hero-worship in his men, he also had their insatiable greed for wider fields and more power.

Another participant in the drama may be considered here. Little attention has been paid to the part played by Irene, Roger's mother-in-law. She was the widow of John-Asen III, King of Bulgaria, and his throne should have passed to her elder son; instead it was usurped by another dynasty. Of course it was conveniently forgotten that John-Asen was himself a usurper, having been foisted on the

Bulgarians in 1279 with Byzantine backing. Irene's brother Andronicus, and indeed the Byzantine empire itself, were too weak to help her win her son's rights. Was her friendship with Roger more than family affection? Was it significant that she and her sons spent the winter with him at Cyzicus?[7] It would surely be plain to a woman of perception that Roger had all the qualities required to put her son in what she would call his rightful place on the throne of Bulgaria (see Table 2, p.18).

We know, too, that Roger was shrewd, far-seeing and ambitious. Did his plans already envisage, not only an empire in Asia Minor, but virtual control of Bulgaria? The Palaeologi could surely not survive between hammer and anvil. And then at last the Roman Empire might be brought to life again. There were no limits to the prizes that another Caesar could grasp; with his resolution and his invincible Almugavars his dreams might become substance. The Mediterranean once more a Roman lake; the Danube frontier secure and in the care of his own brother-in-law. Then to the east! Lands of fabulous wealth could be reached when the Turks had been hurled back to their ancient pastures. Another Alexander might penetrate to the Indus—and beyond. But if his plans were ingenious, there were crafty opponents in Constantinople, cunning and ruthless. Would no one warn him? Could he not sense that there were clever Greeks at court who had some inkling of ambitious plans hatched during the winter evenings at Cyzicus?

With Kula reduced to obedience the Grand Duke returned to Philadelphia, and it is now that he is said to have extorted those contributions to his war chest that were so deeply resented. A certain Nostongos Ducas, one of the higher officials, returned to Constantinople with complaints about the treatment of the citizens; not only had they endured a protracted siege, but now had an army billeted on them, an army with a healthy appetite. Somehow the foreigners had to be fed, even while the citizens were recovering from their prolonged privations, during which even an ass's head had fetched an enormous sum. Ducas began to pour poison into the ear of Andronicus, who refused to listen. Was he really so trusting, or was there some deeper motive in his apparent partiality for Roger? Was he perhaps biding his time, until Roger should have cleared Anatolia of the Turks?

Ducas now approached the Patriarch, ready as ever to listen to the worst about the heretic Latins; he in turn spread the stories among Roger's declared enemies. Then, to everyone's surprise, Andronicus publicly praised the Grand Duke's achievements, declared that the honours he had so far received were not yet consistent with his merits or services, and had Nostongos Ducas taken away to prison. It has not occurred to historians that Andronicus was by no means as foolish as his behaviour suggests; he could dissemble and he could wait.

Meanwhile Roger made sure that the last of the Turkish besiegers had abandoned their strong points round Philadelphia. His strategy was admirable, for he realized that before marching east he must cleanse the west coast of Asia Minor of its Turkish bands. He had already cleared the Hermos valley by taking Kula; now he could march down it to the neighbourhood of Sardis, where Salihli now stands. Going west from there he took the southern branch where the road forks at Turgutlu and entered Nymphaeum or Nif (Kemalpaşa). As the army marched between the lush plantations of figs and pomegranates the men could see a palace on their right; its ruins are still visible.[8] Here Michael Palaeologos, in 1261, had signed the commercial treaty with the Genoese ambassadors, Guglielmo Visconte and Guarnerio Giudice. It enabled him to gain an empire and from it stemmed the Genoese ascendancy and the temporary—only temporary—eclipse of the Venetians, who had divided the spoils of the east with the Crusaders in 1204. Finally a turn southward from Nif enabled the Catalans to clear the Turks from Nyssa (near Nazilli), where the ruins of a theatre and a council chamber are all that survive among the olive groves.[9]

The campaigning season of 1303 was drawing to a close and it was time to seek winter quarters. Magnesia was ideal as a headquarters,[10] but Roger had scarcely dismounted there when an exhausted messenger flung himself from his foundered horse. Alarming news from Tira. The town was closely beset by Turks of the emirates of Meteşe and Aidin; unless immediate help was forthcoming the defenders could no longer hold the crumbling walls. At least the lesson of Kula had been learned and the Greeks were no longer handing over their besieged towns so readily.

With a small, mobile force Roger made a forced march to Tira, covering thirty-seven miles in seventeen hours. He was told that the Turks, whose numbers had been swollen by survivors from Philadelphia, were in the habit of bivouacking in copses some distance from the town and issuing at daybreak to continue their assaults and lay waste the fields.[11] The Catalans arrived at night, when the coast was clear, and entered the town silently. At first light the Turks were massed before the main gate; they knew nothing of the arrival of reinforcements until it swung open and Corberán d'Alet charged out, followed by 200 mounted men-at-arms and 1,000 Almugavars. Once more surprise had given the Company the first advantage; once more the survivors of Philadelphia heard the menacing '*Desperta ferre!*' and in an instant the fierce Almugavars were among them, hacking, stabbing and slitting throats. More than half the Turkish force was killed and the rest, intent only on saving their lives, broke away to the south, where the stony slopes of the Güme Dagi offered some hope of safety.

Corberán followed at the gallop, but the enemy was well mounted and more lightly armed and reached the mountain ahead of the mailed horsemen, in time to abandon their horses and scramble up to a defensible position. Corberán ordered his men, too, to dismount and, with more valour than prudence, himself began to climb the slope, braving stones and arrows in his haste to get to grips with the enemy. As he struggled up in the heat and the swirling dust he found his armour irksome and, intent only on closing with the enemy, threw off his cuirass and shortly thereafter his helmet. His rashness was soon punished; a Turkish arrow pierced his head and his dying body tumbled back to the foot of the slope. His men (they were not Almugavars) lost heart when their leader fell, called off the pursuit and carried away their dead and wounded.

Corberán's death was a great blow to Roger for, young as he was, the seneschal had shown himself to be a gallant and successful leader of men. Even then Roger's daughter, born of the Cypriot lady, was living with her stepmother, Maria, in Constantinople. The ladies were of the same age and the daughter had been summoned as a bride for Corberán, whom Roger treated as a favourite son. The marriage was to have been solemnized at the end of the summer campaign and was intended to cement the bond of friendship between the Grand Duke and his most valued captain. One is reminded of Napoleon's grief 'for the man whom I loved and esteemed the most', when Desaix was killed at Marengo. And just as Roger had kept his daughter for Corberán, so Napoleon had intended Desaix for his step-daughter, Hortense Beauharnais.

They buried him and ten fallen comrades two leagues from Tira, where a church was said to contain the bones of St George, protector of Catalonia. Muntaner described it as the most beautiful he had ever seen. The funeral was sumptuous, with every mark of grief and respect, and the mourners stayed for a week while the tomb was made both rich and beautiful. Today there is no trace of church or tombs.

From Tira the Grand Duke sent a message to Smyrna (Izmir), whence it was relayed to Chios and thus reached Ferdinand d'Aonés. The fleet was to winter at Ania (Kuşadasi). Here, midway between Ephesus and Priene, is a harbour sheltered from western gales by the island of Samos. Another, smaller island lies offshore and, though its present fortress is a Turkish one, there were older fortifications in the days of the Company.[12] The situation is strategically excellent, with easy approaches to both the river Cayster (Kücük Menderes) and the river Maeander (Büyük Menderes). Homer knew these parts and sang of them, comparing the swarming Argive host with 'the many breeds of wingéd birds, geese and cranes and long-necked swans, in an Asian meadow about Cayster's stream, fluttering here and there, exulting in their wings, alighting ever further with a din that makes the meadow sound'.[13] Surely the Almugavars had their own bard, with his own barrack-room ballad, that said in Catalan:

> When 'Omer smote 'is bloomin' lyre,
> 'E'd 'eard men sing by land an' sea;
> An' what 'e thought 'e might require,
> 'E went and took—the same as me.
> (Kipling, *Barrack Room Ballads*)

It is a safe assumption that none of the Company had heard of the Argives, but the Christian associations of Ephesus impressed at least one, the chronicler Muntaner. For to his joy he was deputed to meet reinforcements led by Bernard de Rocafort and to bring their commander to 'the city of Altolloch, which the scripture otherwise calls Ephesus'. Few small country towns have so long a pedigree of names. As it contains the tomb of St John the Evangelist, the inhabitants of the rebuilt sixth-century town called it Hagios Theologos—Saint Word-of-God. Readers may recall the first words of his gospel, 'In the beginning was the word'. The Word, or Logos, was a rare inheritance from Greek culture; strangely enough, it was at Ephesus, about 500 B.C., that Heracleitus propounded his doctrine of the Logos, the divine truth by which all things come to pass. The next name was Aya-Soluk, the nearest the Turks could get to Hagios Theologos. The Italians, convinced that the Turks had derived their name from something western, took its hilltop position into account and called it Alto Luogo, or High Place. This the Catalans readily changed to the equivalent Alto-Lloch. When the Ottoman Turks took the town in 1426 it became Ayasuluk again and thus Selçuk, until in 1922 it was renamed Akincilar. The new name has not caught on with the inhabitants.

Of Ephesus, Muntaner relates (ch. 206) that 'here is the sepulchre in which my lord St John the Evangelist was placed, when he had taken leave of the people and then they saw a fiery cloud, whence they believe that in it his body and soul ascended to Heaven.' And on the tomb each year, on the feast of St Stephen (26 December), which is the eve of the feast of St John, there exudes a manna, that collects as though it had been poured like water, to the height of a handsbreadth, so that by the day's end there is as much as three quarter-ton Barcelona barrels would hold. The manna, he continues, is good for many purposes, and he gives a list of clinical indications, ranging from obstructed labour to peril at sea.[14] Of the other marvels at Ephesus, the great temple of Artemis had disappeared and the brick and stone house of the Virgin was yet to be discovered; but the Grotto of the Seven Sleepers, the tomb of St Luke and St Paul's prison were all open to the sightseer and were presumably visited by the devout Muntaner. It was a commonplace in the Middle Ages to step aside from a military operation and visit a centre of pilgrimage.

Rocafort had arrived at Constantinople with two hundred men-at-arms, fully equipped except for horses, and a thousand Almugavars. He had been one of the original council in Sicily, when the expedition was planned, but was delayed for a reason that every soldier of fortune would understand: he had been in command of several castles in Calabria, when the War of the Sicilian Vespers was amicably concluded, but he refused to hand them over to the Angevins, as stipulated, until his salary was paid up to date. It took over a year for this to be done, but once he was satisfied Rocafort, a bold and experienced leader, brought his men east with no further delay. Unlikely though it may seem, his obduracy in Calabria was to have far-reaching effects on both him and the Company. From Constantinople, on the advice of Andronicus, he took his ships and men to Chios, where he found Aonés about to leave for Ania. He accordingly sailed with the fleet and sent two horsemen from Ania to acquaint Roger with his arrival; there was satisfaction in the ranks of the Company, for the men knew him personally, and his reputation, as well as the size of his reinforcement, was welcome to their diminishing ranks.

Muntaner was asked to take twenty horsemen and meet Rocafort at Ania, bringing him from there to Ephesus, where Roger would meet him. He was careful to take with him a knowledgeable guide, so that they might travel over paths unseen by Turkish eyes; but with all his precautions the little troop had to clear the way with their swords more than once. The meeting was a cordial one, for Muntaner, Rocafort and Aonés had been comrades in the campaign of Sicily and they had much to talk about. Accompanied by 500 of Rocafort's Almugavars, they took two days for the ride to Ephesus, where they were joined by Roger and the whole of his army four days later. Great was their joy on meeting, and great the awards and honours that came to Rocafort; in addition, one hundred caparisoned horses and four months' pay were handed over for his troops. The post of seneschal left vacant by the death of Corberán was awarded to their leader, as well as the hand of the Grand Duke's daughter, who had been ... well, earmarked is a good enough word, women being treated like cattle in their marriage arrangements, for Corberán.

The usual stories of extortion and cruelty were told of the army in Ephesus. To get money they tortured people and cut off limbs and heads; one Macremi was beheaded because he would not, or could not, pay the assessment of five thousand crowns. All the wealth that had come into his hands, in whatever manner, during the campaign of 1303 was sent by Roger to Magnesia, where he posted a guard and determined to make his headquarters in the coming winter. Again we must strike a balance between Greek tales of Catalan atrocities and Spanish tales of Greek slyness and perfidy. We shall find later that the Catalans were regarded as a lesser evil than their French and Burgundian Crusader predecessors. This may, of course, be but faint praise.

And so the winter passed, with ships careened and scoured, arms and equipment looked over and repaired, good food bought or stolen. The leaders planned the daring campaign of 1304; the men gambled and gorged, exchanging the rigours of war for a brief interlude of domestic tranquillity. Roger might well be content. In little more than a year the unemployed ex-pirate had become a member of the imperial family, defeated the Ottoman and Karamanli Turks and liberated the fertile lowlands of Anatolia. But if he was content he was not yet satisfied.

Chapter 4

To the Iron Gates and back 1304

The campaign of 1304 began with another success, an unpremeditated one. The Turks had learned to evade pitched battles and were no longer grouped in hordes that could attempt the capture of important towns. Like many defeated armies they had broken up into groups of guerrilla fighters, who could raid the fertile valleys and retire to remote encampments in the mountains. One such force, under a leader called Sarkan, had the temerity to devastate the fields and orchards round Ania, where the Company was in billets. One afternoon they were spied by the sentries. To see others wasting a peaceful countryside, making a trail of 'blood and fire', as they called it, was too much for the Catalans to bear; this was something they could do infinitely better. Without waiting for orders, or even for their officers, the Almugavars streamed out of Ania and, with primitive tactics, launched themselves against the front and flanks of the Turks. The latter found flight as costly as resistance, for they had to battle past the enfilading enemy in order to get back to the mountains. All day the fight went on, as scattered parties fought their way through groups of Catalans; at sunset these returned to Ania, hilarious at the success of their sortie, leaving 1,000 enemy horse and 2,000 foot dead on the battlefield. They had always had supreme confidence in their fighting ability; now they knew they were invincible.

The unorthodox victory was a happy augury for the next campaign. During the winter the Grand Duke and his captains had planned the march eastward, and with the troops in their present confident mood the undertaking promised well. It would, however, be imprudent to forewarn the Turks and Roger decided to leave with the minimum of delay; six days were allowed for preparation and on the seventh the army moved out of Ania and began its long and arduous march. It was the same force that had conquered so often; with Rocafort's contingent it still numbered about four thousand Spaniards and the allies probably amounted to no more than another 1,000. It had now become the goal of adventurers, criminals and masterless men of all nations, eager to share the ardours and rewards of its campaigns. Numerous foreign names are found in the records of the Company during the next quarter-century, some of them singled out for special mention in the ex-communication of 1335. Of course the majority of these were late arrivals and, to anticipate, were attracted by the Company's later successes; but even at this time a few French names crop up in the chronicles and the rank and file must have had a fair number of foreigners who are never named.

Roger's plan was a bold one. With his small force he intended marching the length of Anatolia, seeking out what bands of un-conquered Turks remained, and thus restoring the whole of Anato-lia to the empire of Byzantium. Whether this was merely a step to acquiring it for himself the reader will be able to judge. At this stage he had no intention of posting garrisons in newly occupied territory; his force was far too small to spare these and, in fact, the guard he had left in Magnesia in charge of the past year's loot was only a token force. His object was to seek out the remaining Turkish forces and, if he was lucky, meet them in a single decisive battle; thereafter the liberated country would be his for the taking.

It is interesting to guess at the route they took.[1] Their contem-poraries merely state that they met no opposition until they reached the Iron Gates in the Taurus mountains, that narrow pass leading from the bare highlands of Anatolia to the fertile plain of Cilicia, to Tarsus and Adana. Schlumberger, one of the more meticulous authorities of the last century, believed that the Company followed 'the old and interminable Byzantine military road, through the valley of the Maeander, the region of Lake Apollonia (Eğridir), Iconium (Konya), Barata, Kastabala and Cybistra'. Others have been tempted to fit them into the tracks of Xenophon's Ten Thousand (who were still 13,000 at this stage), Alexander the Great and the Crusaders.

But their march followed no historical route, at least until they came to Iconium (Konya). Alexander had criss-crossed Asia Minor, well to the south when he visited the site of Attaleia (Antalya), which was yet to be founded, and far north when he passed through Gordium (Yassihöyük), where modern authorities say he did not cut the well-known knot. Xenophon's expedition also took a considerable bend northwards, passing through Ipsus (near Akşehir) and thence down to Iconium. The knights of the first Crusade (Peter the Hermit's rabble hardly got into Anatolia at all, except as captured slaves of the Turks) passed through Dorylaeum (Sarhöyük, near Eskieşhir) and Iconium too.

The Company was therefore the first expeditionary force to move east from the valley of the Maeander. It was a bold move, like all their undertakings, for though it was the shortest, it was also the most arduous journey of them all, especially since the military road had fallen into disuse. They followed the fertile plain as far as the ruins of Hierapolis, where the remains of a Roman necropolis, gates and baths still survive; they passed below the Byzantine fortress on its cliff, where the glittering minerals later gave it the Turkish name of Pammukale, or Cotton Castle. It is true that the strange limestone stalactites remind one of cotton wool, when seen from certain angles; from others they resemble waterfalls, cascades and swiftly flowing streams turned suddenly into ice. There was a town there in the fourteenth century, and the Company may have begun its career of liberation, while its more devout members went to pray in the Church of the Apostle Philip, at the site of his martyrdom. For, according to Greek authors, liberation was accompanied by depredation, and Spanish sources repeatedly mention centres of pilgrimage attracting a crowd of pious soldiers.[2]

Starting in early spring they would have passed between fields pink with asphodel, so profuse that it could be counted in acres rather than blooms; then came the gradual climb among olive groves and vines into the uplands, all golden with gorse and wild fennel, these of giant proportions, as thick as a man's leg and eight feet tall. Under their feet lay the scarlet anemones, harbingers of the great swathes of poppies that would come with April. Of all the lands colonized by the Greeks, Asia Minor is surely the most prodigal of her wild flowers and most generous with her crops, exceeding even Sicily in her bounty.

As they climbed higher they made their way between holly and cistus, pine and wild olive, among which cattle, sheep and goats pastured in the man-made clearings. Before them and to the right rose the craggy peaks of Baba Daği and Honazdaği, the snow still lying thick in their valleys; in this keen air an hour's sunshine releases such perfumes as city dwellers never know; at any step the savour of thyme or rosemary fills the air, rising from the turf which covers the sleeping stones of a dozen civilizations.

Of the march to the Iron Gates Pachymeres wrote that the Greek population of Anatolia, 'in escaping the smoke, threw themselves into the fire'. The Spanish historian Moncada, on the other hand, relates how the Catalans were received with joy, consoled their fellow Christians and animated them in their own defence. They were the first Christian army that the inhabitants then living had ever seen, for Byzantine troops had for many years not ventured into the interior. It is possible that both authorities were correct and that the Company's departure, as well as its arrival, was viewed with relief by the unfortunate Greeks.

And now began the punishing climb through pine forests to the windswept Anatolian plateau, where a single mud village may be passed in a day's march, where sheep huddle round the infrequent waterholes and an occasional camel train looms up through the dust clouds. The mountains lie in vast, crinkled, yellow chains and only in the valleys does a little vegetation follow the course of a stream. The solid, groaning wheels of the ox-carts were not unfamiliar to the Spaniards, whose own land still resounds here and there to their inhuman shriek. They found nothing outlandish in Baris (Isparta), whose woven rugs could only replicate those for which Moorish Spain was famous, and the Almugavars were unlikely buyers of the rose water for which Isparta has been celebrated for centuries. They moved slowly and circumspectly, on the look-out for the main body of the Turks of Aidin and Karaman, with whom they had to come to grips before Anatolia could be considered free. Over the mountain ranges they trudged, men, women and children, mile after weary mile, with an occasional distant glimpse of the lakes of Pamphylia and Pisidia. And every day they encountered fiercer heat and denser clouds of dust.

From the Seljuk fortress on a hill-top they surveyed the prosperous town of Prostanna (Eğridir) and looked out over the lake of Apollonia and its islands. They had now climbed three thousand feet and from here there was another weary ascent over the mountains to Antioch of Pisidia (near Akşehir). Much as the road had been neglected, for Byzantium's famed postal relays had long since ceased to function, the going must have become easier until Iconium (Konya) was reached. Still no Turkish army, nor news of any. Cautiously they turned south-east, skirting the neighbourhood of Karaman, whose emir they had defeated at Philadelphia. Down in the valley before them was a Byzantine town whose name is now forgotten, though its remains are so plentiful that the Turks call it Bin Bir Kilise Deresi, the Valley of a Thousand and One Churches. Barata was situated hereabouts, and Cybistra, which may have been in the foothills of the Taurus mountains, near the present Ulukişla.

With the forbidding range of the Taurus before them, an ideal site for an ambush with its single narrow path through to the southern plains, more than normal caution was ordered. Roger rightly suspected that the Turkish army would be waiting to pounce among the deep defiles and wisely had the area first reconnoitred by his cavalry. And there, hidden among the folds of the mountain, they found the Turkish host, under the same Sarkan whom they had beaten at Ania. Drums and trumpets sounded to arms and the enemy, seeing that their trap was discovered, streamed down to the plain, eager for battle.

The Company was still weary from marching and its position not of the best; but when had it been their custom to refuse battle because the enemy outnumbered them? The Turkish host, according to Muntaner, consisted of 10,000 cavalry and twice that number of infantry. At daybreak, when the armies took up their positions, the odds seemed extravagant, at least when only numbers were considered. To the Christians it seemed a good omen that it was the feast of St Mary of mid-August, the old *vinalia rustica* that has come down from pagan Roman days. It was a cheering date for the Company, for it marks one of Catalonia's favourite festivals, and was so regarded even before the day was dedicated to the Assumption of the Blessed Virgin.

Let me tell of the battle in Muntaner's words, for the Greek writers, perhaps through jealousy, make no mention of this hard fought and decisive contest. You must imagine the scorching heat, the dust haze raised by tramping feet and galloping hooves and the Almugavars' anxious families looking on. This was to be no walkover, and well they knew it; this was the last foothold of the Turks in Anatolia and nothing but total defeat would make them give it up.

Before this battle, and it is reported of no other, the Spanish troops exchanged good wishes, the *enhorabuena*, 'in a good hour', that can be traced back at least to the days of the Cid. They knew that this was to be no easy victory and exchanged their good luck wishes like gladiators or members of a forlorn hope. But back to Muntaner (ch. 207):

> and the Almugavars shouted '*Desperta ferre!*' and straightway
> the Grand Duke with the cavalry went to attack the horsemen
> and Rocafort with the Almugavars to attack the foot. And there
> you saw feats of arms, such as man never saw before. What
> shall I tell you? The battle was mightily cruel; but at last all
> the Franks raised a shout and cried '*Aragó, Aragó!*' And then
> they gained such a victory that the Turks were overthrown;
> and thus they killed and pursued, the pursuit went on into the
> night, and the night made them break off the pursuit. But by
> then there were dead six thousand of the Turkish cavalry, and
> of the infantry more than twelve thousand. And so that night
> the Company made good cheer, for the Turks abandoned all
> their food and beasts.

They made camp the next day and there they stayed for eight days, 'and the booty they took was without end'.

Looking back over the centuries we sense the exultation of these adventurers, successful beyond the wildest of hopes, except perhaps Roger's. In the restricted world of the Middle Ages, they had conquered the equivalent of what today would be a continent. Where would their valour and good fortune lead them now? Were they at last in sight of the land that was destined to be their home? One thing is certain. Amid the hopes and projects that flew back and forth, none dreamed of what the future had in store, of great disasters and greater triumphs, of the strangest inheritance that ever came to a band of mercenaries.

First they looked ahead. Cautiously a party of scouts, followed by senior officers, climbed to the Iron Gates of Cilicia, so narrow in those days that a mule had to be unloaded to pass through the defile. This was the natural and hazardous road by which armies had always passed to invade the fabulous countries of the east. Looking down over the Cilician plain, now the fertile kingdom of Armenia, Roger and his captains held council. There were those who urged that the army should advance still further, through the lands of the friendly, Christian Armenians, to the rich cities of Syria and beyond.

The Armenians had inclined to alliance with the west, rather than with Byzantium, partly because of their proximity to the Latin kingdom of Cyprus. They would thus be all the more disposed to welcome the Company, deliverers from the ubiquitous Turks. Catalan merchants, too, were numerous and only a few months before Raymond Llull, the great Catalan friar, theosophist, politician, poet and eventually martyr, had spent enough time in Little Armenia to write one of his innumerable books. An ardent Crusader, his influence might have persuaded his hosts that the Company could be the spearhead of another attempt to regain the Holy Places. He had, in fact, called for three practical measures to open the pilgrims' route to Jerusalem: an alliance with the Tartars (who had driven the Turks before them); economic sanctions against Syria and Egypt; and the fusion of all the military religious orders, Templars, Hospitallers and the rest, into a single fighting force. He thought of Little Armenia as an advanced base for his scheme, and there were some who would see the Catalan Company as the instrument of Llull's design, though their method of converting the infidel would possibly have been more practical than the suggestions given in Llull's book, *What man should believe about God.*

But Roger overruled the hotheads who wanted to pass through Little Armenia and fight their way to the Euphrates and beyond. The same refusal applied to a fresh crusade. Perhaps it would have been better for him if he had agreed. Muntaner writes that he had already received a message of recall from Andronicus;[3] it is more likely that his ambitions were at the moment confined to the overlordship of Asia Minor and that he was uneasy about the riches which he had left so weakly guarded in Magnesia.

For three days the Company bivouacked at the Gates, under the proud standards of St George and Aragón; after they were lowered no other colours than the crescent of Islam would fly here. They returned to Ania for the winter of 1304 along the route by which they had advanced, over the yellow mountains, across the endless, windswept plains and down the valley of the Maeander. Their journey was faster, for they sent their booty back by sea and their leader wanted to use the glorious month of October for the recapture of Magnesia, which he now learned had been lost by treachery.[4] Its governor, Attaliota, had once before shown hostility to the Catalans, when he was a supporter of Nostongos Ducas; now, believing the

Company permanently lost in the dangerous hinterland of Anatolia, he had captured, imprisoned and killed the Catalan guards and seized Roger's treasure along with the Company's stored booty. Murdered men and rifled chests cried out for retribution and the army took up its positions to besiege the well-defended city.

But Roger was not to see his valuables again, nor open the campaign of 1305, which was to rid Central Anatolia of its Turks. A messenger from Constantinople brought urgent orders for his recall. The Turkish menace was beaten back, but as ever in the last centuries of Byzantium, a new one had arisen. Theodore, the usurper of the Bulgarian throne, had invaded Thrace and was poised to attack Constantinople. Forget our jealousy, our hostility, our slanders! Come back and save us once again!

Another council of war was held, but this time there was little choice. Roger's policy was to have a creature of his own on the throne of Bulgaria; Moncada suggested, as far back as 1620, that the story of Theodore Sventislav's invasion was a lie. If so, it was well thought out, for subtle minds in Constantinople could foresee that this was the lure which could not fail to bring Roger back. It seems plain that the Emperors were aware of Roger's aims, supreme power in Anatolia and a family interest in the throne of Bulgaria; wise after the event, we may even see the beginning of the plot that was intended to destroy the Catalan danger, the minute they had dealt with the menace of the Turks. Be that as it may, the Bulgarian threat was enough to force Roger to break off the siege of Magnesia, while the council decided that the imperial summons could not be ignored.

The army was paraded—in part. The Alani had deserted and the Byzantine auxiliaries had received an imperial command from Michael IX, that they were no longer to obey the Grand Duke; so important was this measure to the Byzantine rulers that the order was issued in the form of an edict with a seal of gold. I wonder why this alone did not alert Roger to his danger. To call him back posthaste in order to repel an invasion, and at the same time to deprive him of those troops who were most likely to be loyal to the empire— where was the logic in such a command? But Roger was in the position of a chess player intent on working out his own attack and oblivious of any threat from his opponent. Thus it happened that only the Catalan Company followed the Grand Duke on his march back to Europe. There were threats and mutterings, for the weary soldiers resented another task, with relatively meagre pay, while their rich savings remained in the hands of a treacherous Greek. But all were resolved to return in spring to be masters of Anatolia.

They marched north along the coast and their ships kept pace with them. This time there was no pretence; the Greeks were to pay for their compatriots' perfidy. Tempers shortened as the weary road lengthened through inundated country and the cold November rains. Governor Macranos, whose lands extended along the banks of the Scamander, was seized, tortured and beheaded by command of the Grand Duke, or Son of the Devil, as the Greeks began to call him. The motive? Roger accused him of abandoning his post; Pachymeres wrote that he would not pay the 5,000 bezants that the Catalans demanded. It can hardly have helped him, in either case, that he was a personal friend of both emperors. Another high official was saved from the same fate only by the intervention of a prominent lady called Gorgo, who personally paid his ransom to the Grand Duke. These are the documented details to survive from what was frankly a progress of freebooters. As they tramped across the windy plains of Troy the scowling troops had no thought of a greater war long past. They were practical business men, like the Catalan merchants who had spread so widely in the Orient, and their anger at the loss of their treasure bred hatred for the whole race of Greeks.

Arrived at last at Lampsacus (Lapseki), on the Asiatic shore of the Dardanelles, they sent a fast galley to Constantinople to ask for the emperor's commands. These, as usual, were designed to weaken the Company's potential for mischief at home. Emperor Michael, who was supposed to be barring the way against the Bulgar, had no wish for the Catalans' support, possibly because there was no Bulgar menace to resist. His stated reasons were that disorders would be inevitable when the Catalans were quartered with other nationalities, especially the Alani under the bereaved and still resentful Gircon. So Andronicus sent his sister Irene and her daughter Maria to advise Roger to cross into Europe with 1,000 picked troops and leave the rest on the Asian shore.

Another council of the Company met and unanimously voted against dividing their force. Then further news arrived; peace had been made with the Bulgars (were they ever at war?) and the Company's officers were alert to the threat of treachery. Irene returned to Constantinople, Maria remained with her husband and the whole

51

army moved across the straits. The town of Gallipoli (Gelibolu) was to be their headquarters and the troops were billeted throughout the historic peninsula, 'the most gracious cape in the world', says Muntaner, 'that has abundance of good bread, good wine and every fruit'. We can only marvel at the Emperor Andronicus that, foiled in his attempt to divide the Company, he should allot them a strategic site, from which they could interrupt his sea-borne traffic with the west. Perhaps he thought the unruly mercenaries less dangerous in a peninsula that could be sealed off.

Roger, with an escort of his best troops, took four galleys and went to attend the emperor in Constantinople. The welcome was enthusiastic, both from the crowd and their sovereign, for the former could not know of Roger's grand design and the latter could dissemble even though, as one writer puts it, 'he hated the Catalans even more than the double procession of the Holy Ghost'.[5] All that the common man knew, as he threw his sweaty cap in the air, was that the mercenaries had repelled the Turkish menace and restored to the empire its richest possession. And as the heroes of Cyzicus, Philadelphia and the Taurus marched by, along the avenues of the 'God-defended City', as it was officially called, the cynic might have said, with Housman,

> Their shoulders held the sky suspended,
> They stood, and earth's foundations stay;
> What God abandoned, these defended,
> And saved the sum of things for pay.
>
> *(Epitaph on an Army of Mercenaries)*

Nor did the exploits of the Company pass unnoticed in the west, and the reaction there must have helped to shape the tortuous policy of the emperors. The Pope, like Ramon Llull, affected to see prospects of the recovery of the Holy Land, but Constantinople numbered him among the robbers who coveted her. The Pope's argument was sound; was this not a Catalan army, and was not their king, James II, Gonfalonier and Captain-General of the Church? Had he not committed himself to taking the Cross? And Charles of Valois remembered his treaty with Frederick of Sicily, the undertaking—a diplomatic gesture, it will be recalled—to help him in a venture to the Levant.

The Genoese, we may be sure, added their quota to the fog of suspicion and the brooding storm-cloud of hostility that now hung over the city. Their spies had brought them the text of a letter from the noble Berenguer d'Entenza to James II of Aragón; to minds already poisoned a certain ambiguity of phrase could amount to an overdose. Some said, with Gregoras, that Entenza had been summoned by Andronicus to offset Roger's ambitions; others believed the Genoese, when they claimed that the King of Aragón was privy to another Latin attempt against Byzantium. With the faultless timing of Fate in a Greek tragedy, the Genoese slander had scarcely been whispered when the Company received reinforcements. Nine Catalan galleys rowed up the Golden Horn; the flagship came alongside the Blachernae wharf. Nobles and commoners gathered to greet the arrival, carpets were spread, garlands woven and down the gangplank, in his finest raiment, with all the proud assurance of a Spanish noble, stepped—Berenguer d'Entenza.

Among the welter of conflicting accounts of Entenza's voyage to Constantinople, Muntaner's story is outstanding for simplicity and verisimilitude. Entenza, a cavalier of noble lineage, and Roger de Flor, the former pirate, had sworn brotherhood while they fought as companions in Sicily; Entenza was present at the council that followed the Peace of Caltabellotta but, like Rocafort, was unable to sail with the Company in the autumn of 1302. That is all. Moncada amplified the tale by adding that Entenza was expecting reinforcements from Catalonia and, as a captain's status varied with the numbers he led, he preferred to await their arrival. At all events he was welcomed by all parties. He had stopped at Gallipoli on his way and renewed old friendships; he was now doubly welcome to Roger for the newly arrived galleys, anchored in sight of the royal palace, were a powerful help in the diplomatic arguments that were proceeding.

The discussions with Andronicus were protracted and much of their content can only be surmised. Greek monks who were contemporary chroniclers drew on their imagination for some of the dialogue, for they cannot possibly have been present. Pachymeres relates that Roger, as usual, asked for more money to pay the new arrivals and that the Emperor coldly asked how it was that the reinforcements had come without an invitation.[6]

'Because,' replied Roger with cool sarcasm, 'they must have heard of your generosity.'

Gregoras, on the other hand, informs us that Andronicus had twice invited Entenza, so that he might play one leader off against the other. A rash decision, if true, for the invitation had resulted in the arrival of another thousand Almugavars, 'Sons of Perdition'.

Roger's main differences with Andronicus were financial. If love of money was the root of his intransigance, or insolence as the Greeks described it, lack of money was responsible for the Emperor's resistance. Roger began by asking for back pay and more besides. Andronicus told him that the imperial treasury was empty, since taxes had not arrived from Anatolia for some years. Roger repeated his demands; Andronicus could think of only two solutions, the resources of the spendthrift and incompetent, devaluation and an increased tax on wheat. The gold coinage had already suffered adulteration more than once and now it was to be further debased, so that only five parts in twenty-three were gold; silver suffered similar depreciation. Roger insisted that his Almugavars wanted 300,000 *bezants* in good money and the opportunity of continuing to earn. He was, of course, fully justified when he told Andronicus that his Byzantine title and dignities only made his troops resentful. They had lost their savings, their pay was in arrears, their future uncertain; why, they thought, should their senior officers, the leaders whom they had elected, flaunt their rank and decorations and live on terms of intimacy with royalty?

The Emperor then suggested that the Company's loot, which in any case was largely spent or lost, should count as part payment; but his Grand Duke countered that no soldier of fortune would listen to such a proposition. The discussions were long and Roger's German blood welcomed the moment when the velvet glove could be taken off and the mailed fist brandished. The Emperor remained outwardly suave. Roger asked for a fief in Anatolia; Andronicus, who presumably was fully informed of Roger's ambitions, was not going to give away his hand by being too accommodating too quickly. He insisted that a large part of the Company first return to Sicily or Spain. This was of course the last thing that Roger could agree to, in view of his ambitious plans; his refusal could only confirm the Emperor's strong suspicions. He pointed out that Roger had already made enemies of the Genoese and Roger replied that he could count on the galleys of Sancho, brother of Frederick of Sicily. It was possibly at this juncture that Andronicus became confidential and hinted at a plan which can only be inferred—by its very nature it would be kept secret—and which is detailed in the next chapter.

Whether because of the bait alluded to in the last sentence, or to

Roger's stronger position for bargaining, he won most of his demands, but Andronicus insisted that the Company swear a new
oath of fidelity. Seldom can a pact have been sworn with less intention of keeping it on either side. Roger was to have the whole of Asia
Minor in fief, subdividing it among his officers in the usual feudal
manner.[7] I may remark, in passing, that this would have deprived
Byzantium of all but a share of her richest territory, of the whole
region from which the Palaeologi had made their spectacular come-
back in 1261. Was there none to warn Roger that his ambitions were
being realized with suspicious ease? There is more than a grain of
truth in the trite saying that success had gone to his head. *Quem
Deus vult perdere prius dementat.*

   In the end Entenza was given the rank of Grand Duke too; some
say that Roger made the gesture of surrendering the title to one
whose blood made him a more fitting recipient. In the event, Roger
was promoted to the greater dignity of Caesar, a title which had been
unemployed for years and was previously reserved for those who
married into the imperial family.[8] This, of course, Roger had done
two years before. Was the selection of the rank of Caesar a part of
the plot to get rid of the Catalans? Had the Emperor guessed that it
would be fuel to the flames of Roger's ambition? Surely he expected
that, as Caesar of the Empire, Roger would burn to emulate the
deeds of the great Julius. He would hardly stop to think that titles,
like the *bezant*, were becoming progressively devalued; a law as
immutable as Parkinson's decrees that an empire's greatness is in
inverse ratio to the number of posts in the civil service. So it happened that as far back as the eleventh century new titles were being
invented as fast as Byzantium was losing territory after the disastrous
battle of Manzikert. *Sebastokrator, protosebastos illustrissimus, pan-
hypersebastos* and *despota* were a few of them, and soon even the resounding *pansebastos sebastos* became so devalued that the holders
were two an obol. At the time we are considering a Caesar was an
official of either the second or third grade, inferior to a *despota* but
well ahead of the *mystikos*, an aptly named civil servant, the *akolou-
thos* or chief of the Varangian guard, who had sunk to the fifty-first
grade, and the great *Tchaouch*, or Master of the Mint. And such was
the rigour of court ceremonial that these splendiferous nonentities
even had to gnash their teeth in silence.

   Entenza's attitude, after the first welcome, had rapidly become
one of distrust. Of noble birth and certainly better schooled than

Roger, he may have remembered Virgil's *'timeo Danaos et dona ferentes'*. The gifts began to arrive after he had refused Andronicus' invitation to a banquet ashore. He carefully remained on board his galley and refused even to visit the Emperor if the latter's son John was not first handed over as a hostage. The Emperor remained polite —Moncada says subservient—and sent him presents and tasty meals from the imperial kitchen. Entenza took his time over returning the dinner service, which consisted of thirty gold and silver dishes. Eventually, and with a great show of reluctance, he accepted the Emperor's safe conduct, with its gold seal, in place of the hostage and presented himself at the place of investiture.

Roger ceremoniously handed his bonnet, staff and standard to Entenza and himself received the insignia of Caesar from the Emperor's hands, his own meanwhile respectfully draped in the folds of his mantle. The trappings were similar to the Emperor's, except that robes and slippers were blue instead of purple. Even his throne was identical, except that it was half a palm's breadth[9] lower. We may guess that Roger's stature made up the difference. Muntaner cannot restrain his satisfaction at the new honour and stresses the fact that the Caesar's throne was nearly as high as the Emperor's. He adds that Roger could now sign himself 'Caesar of our Empire', and the Emperor would write to him as 'Caesar of your Empire'. Such a meteoric rise, in so short a time, would be remarkable in any age; in dramatic effect it is only eclipsed by the suddenness of the fall. 'Who', says d'Olwer, 'would have predicted that the highest rank, too noble for a prince of the blood, would be revived after many years of disuse, for a soldier of fortune, renegade brother of the Temple, pirate and son of a falconer?'[10]

Entenza's official investiture took place at Christmas, but Roger spent most of the rest of the winter in Gallipoli with his wife and her relations. He refused the Emperor's invitations to the feasts of Epiphany and Candlemas, celebrated with great pomp in Constantinople. He had received and distributed the troops' pay, to their general satisfaction; but under the placid surface of their relations there were cross-currents of discontent between the Company and the throne, and between the officers and men of the Company. What good did it do them, asked the Almugavars, that their officers were showered with titles? Were the new Caesar and Grand Duke so flattered by their new honours that they no longer fought for their men's rights? Roger tried to reassure them and Entenza, who had been present at meetings of the Council of State during the winter, decided that he could calm his followers only by returning to Gallipoli. More Genoese whispers made the atmosphere still cooler; he could no longer ignore the hostility around him and he was disgusted with the evidences of imperial vacillation and double-dealing. At long last he returned the gold and silver dinner service which, says one author, he had put to the basest uses.[11] Then, as his galley drew away from Blachernae, he dropped his ducal regalia overboard, in full sight of the palace. 'This action,' says Moncada, 'was the most praiseworthy of all this great cavalier's deeds in the Orient.' He was referring to the business with the regalia, not the dinner service.[12]

Time passed slowly, but at last the winter ended and the moment came to cross over once more into Asia. The order to embark was welcomed by the officers who had their new fiefs to inspect, while the prospect of resuming the siege of Magnesia and recovering their loot sustained the other ranks. The embarkation was proceeding when the last blow fell. The Greeks round Gallipoli were being paid by the Company for the victuals consumed during the winter. The money was that sent by Andronicus to satisfy their demands and the Greeks, more experienced in obliquity than the Catalans, refused to accept it at face value. The Almugavars recognized only one method of argument and soon blood was flowing in the Greek villages. Now there was suspicion and hostility between Greek and Spaniard, between officers and Almugavars, and between generals and emperors. One senses the distant rumble of thunder; the storm was about to break.

Chapter 5

The murdered guests
1305, April–May

The move to Asia had begun. Detachments of the Company were at Lampsacus (Lapseki), Pegües (Karabiga), Cyzicus and Lopadion (near Karacabey); others were still on the European side, waiting to embark, and among them were those destined to be Roger's escort on his last journey to Adrianople. If there was a plot to weaken the Catalan Company and make it vulnerable to the comparatively feeble Byzantine forces, it had now succeeded.

Roger had returned from another visit to Constantinople, where he had taken leave of the Emperor Andronicus. Entenza too had joined the Gallipoli garrison after his somewhat theatrical gesture in view of the Blachernae palace. Some say that his disdainful discarding of the trappings of his grand ducal rank caused fresh anxiety in the imperial breast; were the Spaniards contemplating another *coup de main*, such as that of the fourth Crusade? If this should indeed be the case, Andronicus would feel only a revival of suspicions never completely allayed. Entenza had sensed treachery behind the benign mask of the Emperor. To one not intoxicated with succes there was something suspicious about the handing over of Anatolia in feud to a band of adventurers. I have mentioned the value of the Asian provinces: what was left of the empire, after the partition between Franks and Venetians, was scarcely sufficient to sustain the unwieldy head of Constantinople on its attenuated body.

At the palace there were enough courtiers to remind Andronicus that the Company had taken, not the imperial eagle, but the pales of

Aragon to the borders of Armenia, and that each parcel of land delivered from the Turks was becoming the property of the Latins. The remedy was temptingly at hand. Patriarch and generals would urge Andronicus to act, while the Sons of Perdition were divided between Gallipoli and the shores of Asia Minor. It seems feasible, indeed, that the suggestion was superfluous. One can easily picture a plot going back to the previous year, when Roger was recalled from Magnesia to fight the Bulgarian usurper. Bulgaria, I have suggested, was the magnet that brought him back, leaving his hard-won treasure in the hands of the treacherous Attaliota. If this were the case, then the division of Roger's forces was not an opportunity to be seized but the result of careful planning.

And now, on the eve of his departure for the new fief of Anatolia, Roger announced that he was going to Adrianople to say good-bye to co-Emperor Michael. His family and friends were appalled. Michael's enmity was common knowledge; had he not refused Roger an audience the year before? Was it not Michael who had punished the citizens of Pegües for admitting the Almugavars? Madness, they said, sheer madness. Maria and her mother, the ex-Empress of Bulgaria, begged him on their knees to give up this foolhardy idea. Maria, now pregnant, urged him to show consideration for her and their unborn child, reminding him that he was her only protector amid the dark plots and cruel revenges of the Byzantine court. Roger was adamant. A council of the Company was summoned—a ghost of democracy still survived under the Caesar's rule—and unanimously urged him not to persevere with his journey. He answered them that he must show his loyalty to Michael and bid him a formal farewell, as he had already done to Andronicus. For this ostensible reason, trivial enough in the opinion of his friends, Roger and his escort went to their deaths.

It is strange that his motives have never been subjected to critical analysis. The lovable Muntaner, simple and ingenuous, seems satisfied with Roger's explanation, that he went 'for the great loyalty that he had in his heart, and the love and correct consideration he bore the Emperor and his son . . .'[1] Pachymeres, obviously at a loss to account for the unaccustomed stupidity of 'the Devil's son', suggests that he was attracted by the physical charms of Michael's wife, the Empress Maria-Rikta, sister of the King of Armenia.[2] He does not tell us how Roger intended implementing his evil design in the busy royal palace of Adrianople. Nikephoros Gregoras, equally eager to impute the basest motives, says that Roger went to Adrianople to ask for money and, if it was refused, to take it by force.[3] A curious statement and a strange attempt at extortion when the Caesar's escort, according to the same author, amounted to only two hundred men, while Michael was in command of an army!

Pears suggests that Roger wanted to find out the strength of Michael's army. Why? A half of his own was already in Asia; of what use would the knowledge be, even if he could obtain it? No surprise attack could at this stage be entertained. D'Olwer,[4] a more thoughtful commentator, can think of four possibilities. First, that Roger had no idea of possible treachery, surely an unlikely explanation after his wife and her mother had specifically warned him. Second, that he thought audacity would disarm his enemies; disarm them from what undertaking? Third, that he held cheaply his life, which he had so often staked; it is surely obvious that he had lived for thirty-six years because he had known how to look after himself. Lastly, that he, like Napoleon, had faith in his star; a man so superstitious might have shown less calculation in his previous actions; the explanation might have fitted Corberán d'Alet, who cast away his armour in the heat of battle, but not the prudent Roger. Never in his short but adventurous life had he acted on impulse. No, for a plausible explanation we must explore the scheming mind of a Byzantine emperor, a type that survived by cunning rather than force, the mind of Andronicus, not Michael.

Andronicus was by no means the simple, irresolute man, as so often presented; in his forty-six years on the throne, or off it,[5] his survival entailed the constant exercise of dissimulation and intrigue. Entenza's distrust after their first meeting will be remembered. Andronicus had good cause to feel resentment against the new Caesar; the fact that the Catalans fought with his pay under their own flag was only a minor irritation. More important was the fact that, apart from their exactions and cruelties, they stayed on for years after being engaged on a nine months' contract. Roger had now succeeded in his evident ambition of becoming overlord of Anatolia and Andronicus could guess how long the feudal ties that bound him would endure. I have mentioned that in this matter the Emperor gave in with suspicious readiness, as though he had foreknowledge of Roger's plans and had decided on a permanent solution; western historians record as a fact that the Greeks, repenting of their decision to summon the Catalan Company, thought they would be rid of the incubus by murdering their leader.[6] Again, the Turks had ceased to be a menace, so that the reason for the Company's presence no longer existed; and the Bulgarian usurper Theodore, even if he had really constituted a threat, had now been pacified, having usefully provided the excuse for recalling the Company from Asia Minor. These arguments are admittedly no more than a list of probabilities with varying amounts of factual support. The only one that is mere guesswork is the assumption that, if Roger planned to put his brother-in-law on the Bulgarian throne, the plan would scarcely have remained unknown to, or unsuspected by, Andronicus.

This last assumption, however, provides a credible explanation of Roger's fatal journey. Having resolved to murder him, Adrianople would seem to be the ideal place for the deed. It was far enough away from the rest of the Company and it was the headquarters of a Byzantine army led by Michael. But how to get him there? Andronicus had only to ask himself, 'What will be the most tempting bait?' The answer has been given: Roger's grand design, the encircling of the empire by placing his own brother-in-law on the throne of Bulgaria. Now Andronicus has only to tell Roger that the latest Bulgar invasion has persuaded him that a more friendly ruler of that country is essential; that he has discussed the matter with Michael (who is guarding the approaches to and from Bulgaria) and that they have agreed to restore the rightful heir. This is not only Roger's brother-in-law but the nephew of Andronicus and Michael's first cousin. Could anything be more reasonable? 'Go,' says Andronicus, 'and work out the details with Michael; he is on the spot. With him you can decide when to come back from your fief in Asia and put the plan into operation. *But tell not a soul why you are going.* Not even your wife must know, for once the Bulgarians get wind of our plan its execution will become impossible.'

Once he had swallowed the bait and decided to go to Adrianople, Roger made the necessary arrangement with his usual promptness and returned to Gallipoli forthwith. His wife and her family were sent to Constantinople with an escort of four galleys, commanded by Ferdinand d'Aonés; it had been agreed that Maria should have her child in Constantinople, rather than in Cyzicus, where Roger would have his headquarters.[7] The command of the forces at and around Gallipoli was entrusted to Berenguer d'Entenza, with Bernard de Rocafort as seneschal of the army. Between them they would supervise the move to Asia Minor.

On 23 March the Caesar set off northwards, accompanied by 300 cavaliers and 1,000 infantry, a quarter of the Catalan Company. It was a five-day march, between wheat fields and olive groves, the landscape gay with the multitude of wild flowers with which Greece so often hides the relics of her ancient glory. On the sixth day, as they neared the city, the Emperor Michael advanced to meet the Caesar with due formality and honour, but really, says Muntaner, so that the scoundrel might find out the strength of the escort. The usual hyperbolic and hypocritical compliments were exchanged; the Catalans were billeted in the city and a present of gold coins distributed among them.

A week passed pleasantly, with Michael and Roger holding their daily discussions. And here is an unexpected inference to add to our list of probabilities. What were these discussions? Roger had ostensibly come to take his leave and good campaigning weather was passing while the entertainments went on. Magnesia waited to give up its treasure, fiefs had to be apportioned and Turks prevented from infiltrating into his new territory. There was nothing so momentous about Roger's departure that a courtesy week of leave-taking was required. He was neither royalty nor an ambassador from a distant land with which a treaty had been concluded. On Roger's side the delay was justified by the plan they were hatching, if my guess is correct. Michael's reason was very different and just as sinister. For while the Company was making merry and the Caesar was being royally entertained, messengers were speeding secretly to summon reinforcements; the 5,000 men of Michael's army were considered insufficient to attack 1,300 Catalans. The additional troops included a few thousand Turcopoles (the offspring of Turkish fathers and Greek mothers, largely professing Christianity) and more Byzantine Greeks, among whose officers we read, without astonishment, the name of Nostongos Ducas, released from prison as mysteriously as he had been consigned there. But the spearhead of the projected attack was formed by the Alani, ever vengeful, under their old leader Gircon, eager to liquidate the family feud with Roger's blood.

On 5 April 1305, the eve of Roger's departure, a farewell banquet had been arranged, so that Michael might complete his catalogue of treachery by murdering his guest, not only in his home but at his own table. The banquet was sumptuous and spirits were high. It may have been a formal occasion at which the diners, not counting the Emperor, had to number seventy-seven; at the top table would be Michael, Roger and four of the most important guests, the remainder being seated in strict order of precedence at a second table, clergy, officers, Catalan guests and palace functionaries. Some say that the empress, Michael's wife, was also present, but this would have been contrary to the usual custom.

When the banquet was at least over, Michael withdrew, leaving the guests more freedom to continue their convivial evening. Gone was the cloud of suspicion that had hung between Greeks and Latins; Roman pledged Catalan while good fellowship reigned through the hall. Suddenly, at a prearranged signal, the doors flew open and the hall filled with Alani, swords and daggers drawn. The unarmed Catalans, surrounded and outnumbered, perished to a man; Roger was killed by a sword thrust in the kidney, delivered by Gircon himself. Blood had repaid the debt of blood. But the murderers were not yet satisfied; so carried away were they by their blood lust that they hacked and hacked at the bodies before tearing them to pieces. Roger's headless, limbless torso is described as left lying on the table amidst used dishes and overturned cups. So perished Roger de Flor, the brilliant and unscrupulous victim of a still more unscrupulous employer. Authors have added details without taking away from the foulness of a deed that is rightly abhorrent to savages. The prurient Pachymeres puts the scene of Roger's death in the bedroom of Queen Maria-Rikta, 'whither he had gone without an escort to take his leave', and adds that he fell at the foot of her bed, pouring torrents of blood, some of which soiled her nightgown. He infers that the leave-taking was somewhat unconventional.[8] When they brought the news of the massacre to Michael, in his private apartments, he is said to have remarked, 'What a pity!' and left it at that.

At the moment when the assassins burst into the banqueting hall the rest of the Alani, Turcopoles and Greeks poured into the town of Adrianople, hunting down the scattered Almugavars and killing or capturing, not only them, but all the Catalan merchants on whom they could lay their hands. Sixty of Roger's escort were seized and thrown into the castle dungeons, where they lay for months, subjected to the worst indignities and in daily expectation of death. They were not to be disappointed. In the end only three of the 1,300 Spaniards survived; they took refuge in a church, where sanctuary availed them nothing. Retreating step by step, keeping their enemies

at their sword points, they reached the stairway of the bell tower.
Here they defended themselves so heroically against the mob and a
detachment of the 9,000 troops who were hunting down their companions that Michael, impressed by their courage, promised them
their lives—and even kept his word. Their names are recorded and
one of them gives the title to the heroic poem 'Roudor de Llobregat',
by a modern Catalan.[9]

The plot had been laid carefully and its scope was wide. Roger's
murder was of course the essential feature, but others were not overlooked. The same night a large party of mounted Alani and Turcopoles was sent off at top speed to Gallipoli, where, finding the
Catalans all unsuspecting, they were to glut their envy and hatred.
The Company's horses were out at pasture and their guards scattered at their ease among the farms; the former were rounded up
and driven away, the latter murdered piecemeal. A thousand men
were thus killed and the combined army and navy at Gallipoli reduced to 3,307, and their horses to 206. The figures are those of
Muntaner, quartermaster of the Gallipoli camp and a careful
accountant.

The news of Roger's murder and that of his companions came as
a shock to the main force. But if the emperors thought that it would
dishearten the survivors they were to learn in a painful way that the
Spaniard fights the more savagely in proportion to the wrongs he
suffers. Apart from some local reprisals, a mere foretaste of what
was to come, the Company behaved with dignity. An embassy was
formed, consisting of a knight named Siscar, the *adalid* Pedro
López, two Almugavars and two sailors, a party representative of
every branch of the force.[10] At the same time a message was sent
to the Doge and Council of Ten in Venice, Genoa's implacable
enemy, informing them that the Company was at war with the
Empire of Byzantium. Siscar's embassy carried a cartel of defiance
in the form commonly used by gentlemen of blood and coat armour.
The challenger took Roger's titles on himself and the cartel began
boldly, if inaccurately, 'Berenguer d'Entenza, by the Grace of God
Grand Duke of Romania, Lord of Anatolia and the Isles of the
Empire . . .' There followed a list of the Company's grievances and
the customary challenge of the day, offering to fight 'ten against ten
or a hundred against a hundred'. The Catalan envoys read out the
indictment to Andronicus, in the presence of representatives of the

various Frankish communities; the Emperor answered that Roger's murder was none of his doing. It is true that his part in it is only a matter of conjecture but there is little doubt that he now ordered the killing of all Catalans resident in Constantinople, including the admiral of the Company's fleet.

Ferdinand d'Aonés had married the daughter of a Byzantine official, Raoul the Fat, and to do so had adopted the Greek Orthodox religion. He was on good terms with Andronicus, but none of these advantages availed him, for the mob attacked his father-in-law's house, where he was staying, and ignored even the pleadings of their own Patriarch, Athanasios. At the risk of his life the old prelate tried to reason with the attackers, who were butchering every Catalan, soldier or civilian, whom they could find. The story was spread about that Aonés had hidden fifty Almugavars in one of his galleys. Now there was no more hope of restraining the crowd. In vain had the Patriarch risked his life before being hustled away and vainly too did Raoul try to protect his family: all of them, with his son-in-law Aonés, perished in the flames of his burning house. In this the Byzantine rabble was behaving as it had always done. From the sixth century, when the Emperor Justinian had almost fled from its fury, it had been known for its violence. Brought up on such spectacles as public torture and execution, and even encouraged to take part in them, their cruelty against helpless victims was matched only by their cowardice in the face of resolute opponents.

The national uprising against Catalan groups and settlements in every part of Greece, as soon as the inhabitants learned of Roger's death, was so prompt as to suggest premeditation. The Emperor naturally disclaimed responsibility for the murders but the fate of the Catalan embassy persuaded even the kindly Muntaner that Andronicus was a prime mover in the widespread massacre. Siscar's party, their challenge duly issued, asked for a safe conduct during their return to Gallipoli and this was granted, along with an escort. When they reached Rodosto (Tekirdağ), however, the escort joined the population in overpowering the Catalans. With a barbarity singular even for those times, the embassy, its servants and some local Catalan traders, twenty-seven persons in all, were taken to the public slaughterhouse and there quartered alive, their various parts being hung up for the edification of the inhabitants. There seems little doubt that the atrocity was carried out by Andronicus' orders and that the murder of an official embassy, travelling under safe conduct, is but one among many examples of Byzantine treachery.

The attempt to get rid of the Company by murder and terrorism was ill-judged. The immediate reaction of the survivors was not one of panic and headlong flight, but of cold, relentless rage. These men could not be cowed, even by odds of a hundred to one. Deprived of their leaders and many of their companions, reduced in number, hearing daily from the Catalan refugees who were now arriving of massacres throughout Greece, they became doubly dangerous. So far roistering, rape and robbery had been the normal behaviour of any Free Company towards it ally. Now the Catalans were declared enemies and desperate ones at that; henceforth they lived only for revenge. But for this they had to remain alive and their survival entailed unsurpassed heroism as well as unheard-of ferocity. Typically, the simple solution of sailing away with their booty did not occur to them; we shall see what happened when it did.

Within a few days a Byzantine army came in force to attack them. The host of Turcopoles, Alani and Greeks numbered 14,000 horsemen and 30,000 foot, at least according to Spanish sources. Against them Entenza commanded an amphibious force of 3,000 odd, all that remained of the original expedition and the reinforcements that he and Rocafort had contributed. A fosse had been hastily dug, to contain the town and suburbs of Gallipoli, and for the next two weeks the defendants were kept hurrying from one part to another, repelling assault after assault. An indication of their desperate straits is given by Muntaner, who was of course one of the defenders, for this is the only occasion on which he mentions that the garrison even entertained the possibility of defeat, as they ceaselessly defended the fosse.[11]

In the third week of May the Council of the Company met in order to hear a proposal of their leader, Entenza. He spoke to them of their afflictions and reminded them that the worst of hardships was to be persecuted and killed by the very men who should be their allies. 'To retire now,' he told them, 'without obtaining satisfaction for so many crimes, would be unworthy of our name and the fame we have upheld for so many years. Neither kinsmen nor friends would receive us at home, nor would our country acknowledge us as her sons if we did not embark on vengeance and cover our injuries with a veil of the enemy's blood.' He went on to remind them that help from Spain or Sicily would be tardy, if it arrived at all, and made a proposal which is unique for sheer audacity (Moncada, ch. 30):

> Our only hope now lies in these ships and galleys of ours, with which we may attack the enemy where they are weakest, win treasure and replenish our food stores, which are already low. The coasts of these parts support a population without a care, convinced that our forces are insufficient to defend Gallipoli, let alone undertake a raiding expedition. This gives us the chance of creating a diversion and thus reducing the number of the besiegers, as well as inflicting much damage. As I am the proposer of this measure I shall also be its leader.

Could anything be more eloquent of the Company's spirit? Attack, always attack; there are ships and galleys, but at this juncture, when the Catalans were at the lowest ebb of their fortunes, the thought of using them for flight is not even discussed.

Then it was the turn of Seneschal Rocafort, the captain risen from the ranks, and as he spoke his face became flushed and his voice strident with passion. A rough soldier of fortune, he added to the virtues and vices of the Almugavars an imagination and an intelligence far above the normal. Perhaps for this reason he was unduly sensitive to fancied slights and resentful of nobler birth and breeding. Up to a point he agreed with Entenza: 'Our fame would diminish and be lost when we return to our country if our vengeance is not as terrible as the treachery of the Greeks. But I must join issue with Berenguer d'Entenza in regard to his tactics. Dividing our forces strikes me as a cardinal mistake, seeing that as we stand we are already far inferior in numbers and strength. And who can guarantee that, while Entenza is roaming the seas, we shall not be overwhelmed by the besiegers? And where will he then land his booty and shelter his fleet, when there is not another friendly port this side of Sicily?' In this uncertainty, he continued, the troops would have misgivings and feel the breath of fear, even though (and here the commoner cannot resist tilting at the aristocrat) Entenza's breeding and noble deeds are sure pledges of the courage of the nobly born. Rocafort's advice, in short, was to sally out in force and stake all on a pitched battle, anticipating by centuries the famous '. . . how can man die better, than facing fearful odds?'

The majority of the Council voted with Rocafort, but Entenza brushed aside the verdict and in his role of supreme commander began preparing for the raid. By this action, in my opinion, he determined his eventual fate, for although he might be within his rights in overriding the verdict of the Council, he staked his own reputation on the result of his project. It seems as though danger had made both leaders more overbearing than usual, though Entenza's aristocratic blood renders him immune from the criticism of the chroniclers.

And now at last there seemed to be a turn in their fortunes, with the arrival of Prince Sancho Pere (Peter), brother of King Frederick of Sicily, and ten galleys. He was resting at Mitylene but hurried to Gallipoli when he heard of the war against the Greeks. Heartened by his arrival the Council resolved to send an embassy to Sicily, to swear fealty to the king and implore his help in the task of carving out a new addition to his kingdom. Sancho Pere asked Entenza's permission to accompany him on the raid, bringing with him his own ten galleys, and the offer was accepted gladly. But when the time came and the troops began to embark, Sancho Pere changed his mind; the ostensible reason was that Sicily and Byzantium were not at war, a nugatory excuse, for in accordance with the international law of those days one party to a truce could assist the enemy of the other party.

The general opinion was that Sancho Pere was unworthy of his father, Peter the Great, and Entenza practically wrote as much in a dispatch to Sancho's eldest surviving brother, James II of Aragón. But the Almugavars shrugged and went on with their embarkation; dawn landings, the clash of arms, throats to cut and plunder to be won, that was their idea of a man's life. And they knew that they represented the pick of the Company, leaving Rocafort and Muntaner to command five knights and 1,462 fighting men. 'And thus,' says Muntaner, 'we remained in such straits that every day from Matins to Vespers we had to battle with those outside.'

It was now, as they ceaselessly defended the fosse, that the refugee Catalan merchants began to show their worth; not only could they fight, but they could trade, and once the garrison had survived the initial onslaught the merchants were able to enrich their fellows by using the huge store of loot for further trading. Strangely enough, there is no mention at this juncture of the Almugavars who had already crossed to Asia Minor. Did they return to support their beleaguered comrades, and if so, in what vessels?

Chapter 6

The vengeance begins
1305, May–December

We have seen how mistaken was the belief that the murder of Roger would tame the Catalans; the news of the massacres at Rodosto and Constantinople inflamed them even more, if that were possible. They felt bereaved and friendless and from now on they lost no opportunity of avenging Byzantine treachery on every Greek whom they encountered. Entenza sailed east to the island of Marmara, which lies due north of the Artaki peninsula. He landed his fifty horsemen and 800 Almugavars and sacked every town, village and farmstead, beheading the inhabitants without exception, men, women and children. What was not worth taking away was burned or otherwise destroyed, so that they left not a living creature, nor any growing thing of value, when they sailed away. This was a fore-taste of the Catalan vengeance, whose memory is still alive; total war in which destruction rather than loot was the chief aim.

All along the north coast of the Sea of Marmara they spread the same devastation, until they reached the strong and wealthy city of Heraclea; Muntaner calls it Recrea, but there is no room for con-fusion if ancient maps are consulted. Today there is no trace of it, though it must have lain near the village of Marmaraereğlisi; it cer-tainly survived the Catalans, for it was sacked again by the Genoese in 1351. Unhappy land! We can guess why opposition to the Turks in the following century was only sporadic. Heraclea was only fifty miles from Constantinople and bad news travels fast; Andronicus heard of its complete destruction when he had just been assured that

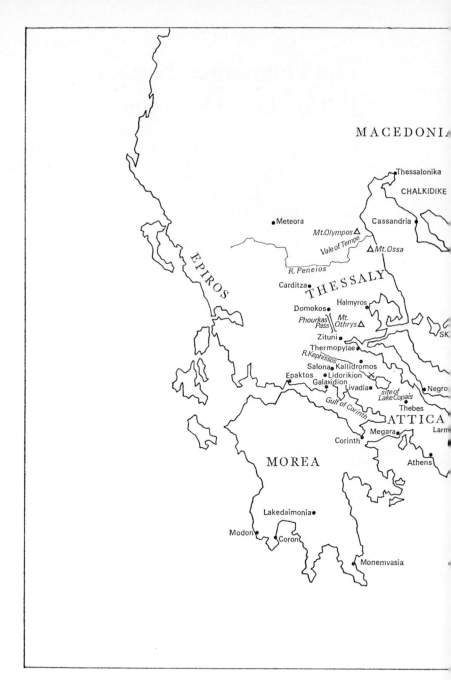

Map 2   Thrace and the Sea of Marmara

BLACK
SEA

Mt.Hermos △

● Pamphylia

● Adrianople

Bizia ●

e △

THRACE

Apros ●

Ponte Regia

Sthenia ●

topolis

Rodosto ●

Constantinople

THASOS

Heraklea

Nona

Megarix

MARMARA

Brachialium ●

Artaki
Peninsula

Athos

Pegües ●

Cyzicus ●

Gallipoli

Madytos ●

ANATOLIA

● Izmir

Karystos ●

TENOS

MYKONOS

CYCLADES

NAXOS

RHODES

F

the Company had sailed away to Sicily to seek safety. He immediately ordered one of his sons, Kaloioannes, to take 400 horsemen
and what infantry he could collect and oppose further depredations
by Entenza. The latter, instead of taking to his ships, landed all his
men again and offered battle to the Greeks, who were amazed that
he should prefer fighting against superior numbers to sailing away
with his booty. The battle was fought at Ponte Regia (Çorlu), where
a Roman bridge from the Via Egnatia still survives. Once more
valour and discipline prevailed. The army of Kaloioannes melted
away and their leader just managed to escape with his life; he returned hurriedly to Constantinople, where Andronicus, having sent
the last of his home guard against Entenza, was forced to arm the
citizenry.

The Catalans' next move was obvious; against the feeble resistance that could be expected in Constantinople, Entenza's men confidently expected another victory and their intention was to destroy
ships and harbour-works in the God-defended city itself. But before
they could implement their plan the Almighty deputed His work to
the Genoese. At daybreak of 28 May the Catalans espied eighteen
sail to the west, so placed that they cut the line of retreat to Gallipoli.
They adopted a common defensive manœuvre, beaching their vessels
in the shape of a fan, with their prows close together on shore, and
manning the aftercastles, the most readily defended part. The
Genoese approached and sent an officer to invite Entenza on board
the flagship, where he could discuss matters of mutual interest with
their admiral, Edward Doria. Just as Roger went trustingly to his
death, so Berenguer d'Entenza, the man who would not set foot
in Constantinople without a hostage, accepted the Genoese safe-
conduct and went aboard their flagship. He and his escort were well
received, dined and persuaded to sleep. When they awoke they
found themselves prisoners and the Genoese fleet making ready to
attack their own. Four of the Catalan galleys were quickly overrun,
unprepared as they were, with the loss of two hundred Genoese; the
fifth, however, had a little time to get ready and met the assault of
the eighteen Genoese galleys with resolution. Its commander was
Berenguer de Villamarín, scion of a famous family of sailors and an
earlier Sir Richard Grenville. He and his crew died to a man and the
Genoese lost another three hundred killed and many wounded.

It is strange how trusting the Catalans continued to be in the face
of repeated breaches of faith. Like other primitive people it never

occurred to them to break their word or assault a guest. Nor could they accustom themselves to such infamy perpetrated by other nations. Their vices were brutality and greed; in their 'virtues' they had not subsumed craft and perjury. The same could later be said of the American Indians. Roger had been shrewd, but even Roger was outwitted by more blatant treachery; and in any case, Roger was not a Catalan. In the whole of this story there is not one instance of the Catalan Company breaking its word or the laws of hospitality, even in the accounts of the hostile Greek chroniclers. Let us remember it when we pass judgment.

'So Berenguer's journey came to this tragic end,' says Moncada; 'an expedition badly conceived, well executed and worthy of better fortune . . . Among the captains discussing the foray, there was talk of the various risks they would run and though these were many and various the actual event was neither imagined nor foreseen.'[1] Entenza was taken to the Genoese quarter of Pera in Constantinople. There was an immediate bid from Andronicus, who offered 25,000 *perpres*[2] for the prisoner; the Genoese did not wish to risk the enmity of the King of Aragón by delivering one of his noblest subjects to the revenge of the Greek emperor; furthermore, they had not long since refused to accept a quantity of depreciated Byzantine coins and were even less enthusiastic about accepting money from the same source. To make sure that they would not lose the prisoner, they sent him to the Genoese trading station at Trebizond and later put him on a ship sailing for Genoa. As they passed down the Dardanelles Muntaner was allowed to visit the prisoner. He offered a ransom of as much cash as could be collected, namely 5,000 *perpres*; the Genoese again played for safety, considering that Andronicus might well withdraw their trading privileges if they gave such a valuable prisoner back to the Catalans. Muntaner's pleading was unavailing and he had to content himself with giving Entenza 500 *perpres* to buy luxuries during his forthcoming imprisonment in Genoa, and assured him that representations would be made to the Genoese government through the kings of Aragón and Sicily.

Back in Gallipoli the Council met again to review their position, which was graver than ever. They had lost both their original leaders, Roger de Flor, and his successor, Berenguer d'Entenza, with many of their best officers. Ferdinand d'Aonés had also been murdered, and their original seneschal, Corberán d'Alet, killed in battle. The garrison was now reduced to 1,200 infantry, 200 cavalry and six officers; Rocafort was now supreme commander and Muntaner appointed governor of Gallipoli and quartermaster of the forces. They still had four galleys, twelve armed freighters and a two-decker, with a number of pinnaces and other small craft.

The first proposal put before the Council was that a headquarters be established on the island of Mitylene (Lesbos), Gallipoli abandoned and the new base used to send out raiders against the coasts of Greece. Their final decision, and few dissented, was typically Spanish and displayed a nobility unexpected in these rude soldiers. 'Men of such renown,' they resolved, 'must avenge on the spot the betrayal and death of their leaders.' At this low ebb of their fortunes, Muntaner continues, the small group of survivors decided to scuttle their ships and to treat as a coward and traitor any who disagreed with this project.[3] We know that the Almugavars would in any case fight to the death; cutting off their retreat determined that the least resolute of their companions too would fight like cornered wild beasts. The same action was taken by the Sicilian Agathocles in 310 B.C., but in his case he had the support of 30,000 fresh troops, whom he had landed in North Africa during the war with Carthage. The only really comparable act of heroism was that of Cortés, who faced mutiny when he scuttled his ships in the harbour of Veracruz. That was 200 years later, possibly inspired by the Catalan Company's example and attended by the same success. Like Moncada, I see no reason to debate which were the more heroic, Cortés or the Catalans. 'All were Spaniards,' he says, 'let them share the glory.'[4]

Once the die was cast the Company settled down coolly to put its affairs in order. A council of twelve was elected, to act in concert with Rocafort, who was obliged to follow their advice if it conflicted with his own. Entenza's arbitrary behaviour had at least taught them a lesson. With due solemnity Muntaner then had the banner of St Peter hoisted over the castle keep, for was not James of Aragón standard-bearer of the Holy See? Three more were made ready, the banners of St George, of Catalonia and of Sicily. By these tokens they would show that the pales of Aragón and the black eagle of the Hohenstaufen were to prevail against the golden, two-headed eagle of the Palaeologi. Then they had a great seal cut, their emblem of respectability, with St George on the obverse and the shield of Catalonia on the reverse; the inscription is still clear on documents that survive to this day: *Sigillum felicis exercitus Francorum in*

Romania parti comorantis.[5] To call themselves 'fortunate' or 'success-ful' was at this stage premature; perhaps the word *felix* was used as in Henry V's 'We few, we happy few, we band of brothers.' The use of the word 'Franks', by the way, argues that the name of Catalan was already disliked in countries other than the Byzantine empire. The dog had been given a bad name; it would try to avoid being hanged.

On 7 June the survivors of the Catalan Company made ready for battle. They knelt in the square before the castle, over which the banner of St Peter was waving, said a brief prayer and invoked the Blessed Virgin. Almost before they could begin the Salve Regina, with devout if confused voices, as Moncada puts it, a cloud came up and drenched them in the short time it took to complete the hymn, then vanished as suddenly as it had appeared. They took this as a favourable omen. The enemy had left part of their forces to guard their camp at Brachialium, on the north side of the peninsula, and came with 8,000 horse to do battle. Though the minutest details are available, such as the name of each standard-bearer, we may pass them over; the battle was merely one more illustration of the triumph of valour and discipline over numbers. The armies came together with such a crash that observers in the town of Gallipoli thought that an earthquake had occurred. In a short time the Greeks, whose ranks had been thrown into confusion, began to retreat to Brachialium to reform their ranks. The hot pursuit of the Catalans met a check here, for fresh Greek troops were available and came out to protect their fleeing comrades. With another tremendous on-rush and a thunderous roar, 'Aragón! Aragón! St George! St George!' these too were put to flight. The battle had lasted since sun-up and the pursuit went on till dark, the whole twenty-four miles of the way studded with the slashed bodies of the enemy.

See now how the Company has changed its habits since the days of its conquests in Asia Minor. There the enemy's flight was the signal for looting to begin; here the Vengeance demanded that every Greek who could be overhauled should pay a part of the communal debt with his life. In a desperate effort to escape their tormentors the fugitives made for the shore, and scrambling on to the anchored boats without orders or discipline overturned the greater number and were drowned. Even then, though it was midnight and the battle and pursuit had lasted since dawn, the tireless Catalans were among them, stabbing at those who had not yet been thrown into the sea. Still the Almugavars ignored the lure of valuables, until every available Greek had been killed.

But it was not in their nature to despise the booty, once their vengeance had been meted out to every living enemy. On the following day they returned to the abandoned Byzantine camp and helped themselves to rich apparel, jewels and, perhaps still more important, 3,000 cavalry chargers. The casualties are given as 26,000 on the Greek side and three among the Catalans. *Credat qui vult*. To make the incredible easier to believe, Moncada cites the parallel case of Agathocles, who, having also burned his boats, killed 30,000 Carthaginians, including their commanding officer, for the loss of only two of his men. Both examples are of interest as showing the long ancestry of today's war communiqués.

That was on 7 June. The Thracian Chersonese, as Gallipoli peninsula was called, now lay at the mercy (a badly chosen word) of the Company. From all sides Greek refugees began to pour into Constantinople; from a distance the stream of country folk, their carts loaded with what they had saved from their homes, resembled armies of ants; behind them they left their deserted fields, heedless of the standing crops and the stores of grain they were abandoning. The Catalan Vengeance was on their heels.

The emperors now decided on a supreme effort to defeat the remnants of the Company, of whom they had reckoned to be rid as soon as they had disposed of Roger de Flor. Their last reserves were hastily mustered under the leadership of Michael and placed between the Catalans and Constantinople. The Company had passed a busy day in their usual activity, the destruction of every living creature and all trace of human endeavour. At nightfall they encamped on the slope of a low hill near the village of Apros; shortly, one of their scouts ran in with the news that many camp fires were burning on the far, or eastern side of the same hill. The wish of the majority, to fall on the unprepared Greeks there and then, was overruled by Rocafort and the Council, who preferred to await more precise information of the enemy's numbers and dispositions.

At first light they ordered their ranks, made confession (in a surprisingly short time, in view of their record), took Holy Communion and marched to their appointed stations. As they were so few the infantry was kept as a single body and the cavalry formed into three squadrons, one on each flank and one in reserve. Michael, whose army had been reinforced during the night, could not believe that a mere 3,000 of the Company intended fighting his huge force; he was as incapable of learning as a Bourbon. He soon realized, however, that they had not come over the hill with the intention of surrendering. He hurriedly arranged his troops in a somewhat complicated order of battle, contrasting with the simple array of the outnumbered Catalans. The infantry was divided into five battalions, under Michael's uncle Theodore; on the left wing Michael stationed the cavalry of the Turcopoles and Alani and on the right the picked squadrons of Thrace and Macedonia, with Wallachs and other volunteers, under the orders of the Grand Heteriarch. Michael himself took command of the rearguard, or reserve, accompanied by his brother, the Despot Sennacherim Angelos.

This time it was the Byzantine army which advanced, and the Catalan Company that awaited their onslaught. The charge of the Alani and Turcopoles was received by the Almugavars, 'and they stood like a tower, no man yielding to any',* says Pachymeres.[6] After the first shock the Alani and Turcopoles turned their horses' heads and made off. This uncovered the left flank of the infantry, which was left in the storm like a ship without mast or sails. Rocafort immediately ordered the opposing right squadron of the Company's cavalry to dismount, for many of them were infantry and sailors who had only recently obtained horses; dismounted, they ran into the unprotected flank and engaged the enemy hand to hand, while the main battle of the Almugavars closed from the front. The battle field was soon cleared of all Byzantine troops except the right wing under the Grand Heteriarch. For a considerable time it resisted the cavalry charges of the Catalans, giving the reserve an opportunity of joining them. But hardly had they done so when the Almugavars, having helped to roll up the left flank, arrived at their now unprotected side and broke into their ranks, their javelins and short swords doing frightful execution. Michael played the man that day; his charger became unmanageable and refused to enter the mêlée, but he mounted another, encouraging his own squadron and heartening others who were about to break away. He had scant success and soon found himself and his staff officers alone in the path of the advancing Almugavars. Turning to his remaining companions, 'Now is the time,' he cried, 'friends and comrades, when death is better than life, and life more cruel than death itself. Die gloriously, rather than live with reproach!'

* Καὶ εὐθὺς πύργος ἦδαν ἐκεῖνοι, μηδέν μηδενί καθυπείκοντες

77

Only 100 followed him as he spurred his charger into the ranks of
the Company, but so valiantly did they carry themselves that they
all but reversed the decision of the day. Michael himself killed two
Spaniards and wounded others; then a Catalan sailor called
Berenguer, who had joined the cavalry when he found a fine horse
and new weapons after the previous victory, charged against them
so boldly that Michael took him for some famous captain. He may
have been surprised, even in the heat of the battle, to see his opponent without a shield; but it was the sailor's first battle on horseback
and he had not yet learned to manage mount and arms as well. At
their first encounter, Michael wounded him in the left arm;
Berenguer turned in a flash and with a blow of his mace shattered the
co-Emperor's shield, wounding him in the face. At the same
moment another Almugavar stabbed his horse and Michael would
have been captured there and then, had not his bodyguard come
valiantly to the rescue, one of them dismounting to hand over his
charger and thus heroically meeting his death. Bravery was not the
monopoly of the Catalans. Still trying to turn back and charge the
enemy, Michael was led away by his companions, shedding tears of
rage and shame, until they reached safety in the castle of Apros. The
rout was now complete and, although the Catalans were too few to
venture in pursuit against a possible ambush, they remained masters
of the field.

The moral effect of their victory was considerable. The stream of
refugees became a river, and even the inhabitants of the Genoese
suburb of Pera did not consider themselves safe. Night and day they
thronged at the city gates and Constantinople became so crowded
that the refugees and their beasts camped in the open along the
streets. 'From that hour onward,' says Muntaner, 'the whole of
Romania was defeated and such panic possessed them that one
could not cry "Franks!" but that they thought of instant flight.'[7]
Andronicus had only one thought, to preserve the little that was left.
He made overtures of peace; he asserted emphatically that he had
had no hand in Roger's murder; his embassies offered almost un-
limited money if only the Catalans would resume their alliance,
while at the same time he approached the Genoese, imploring their
aid against the advancing destroyers. But the Catalans had profited
by their experience; unmoved by threats or bribes, they followed the
Vengeance to which they now gave their fanatical devotion. The
embassies came back with empty hands; Rocafort led his troops on

the road to Constantinople, to the sound of trumpets. One would imagine that the city, after the defeat of its last army at Apros, would quickly fall to the Catalan Company. Here we meet for the first time one of its inherent weaknesses: invincible on the battle-field, they were helpless before a fortified city. Cavalry and light infantry, untrained and unequipped for siege warfare, had their limitations.

A sequel to the battle of Apros happened in Adrianople, where sixty of Roger's original escort still remained alive in prison. When the news of the victory arrived they made a supreme effort to regain their freedom. With bars wrenched from the windows they attacked the door of the tower in which they were imprisoned, but to no avail. The townsfolk gathered and a siege began. The Catalans re-pelled all attempts at storming their prison but on the other hand could have no hope of breaking out. Finding their efforts to dislodge the Catalans unsuccessful, the besieging mob, wounded and weary, decided to set fire to the tower. Even with the flames licking round them the prisoners continued to fight with stones and any other weapons they could contrive; then, when the heat and smoke made further resistance impossible, they embraced, bade each other fare-well and, making the Sign of the Cross, threw themselves into the burning pit. There was one exception, a youth who contemplated giving himself up; his companions, to save him from such disgrace, themselves cast him down into the fire.

This old world of ours has seen so much perfidy and bloodshed that perhaps it is not surprising to find the same events enacted in England in the days of King Alfred's son. For Catalans read Danes; for Byzantines, English. Sigefirth and Morkere, Danish envoys, were invited to a banquet at Oxford and were there slain. As to their followers, 'Into the tower of St Frideswyde they were driven, and as men could not drive them thence,' says William of Malmesbury, 'the tower was fired and they perished in the burning.' The strangest part of the episode in Adrianople is that it appears in the chronicle of Pachymeres, and not in that of their fellow-countryman Muntaner. It is the only occasion on which the Greek monk writes of the Cata-lans with admiration.[8] It is probable that Muntaner remained in ignorance of the event, indeed of the fact that some of Roger's retinue had survived the initial massacre, but it is also possible that he regarded it as normal behaviour for Spaniards, who had shown the same contempt for death at Saguntum and Numantia.

Though the larger cities remained safe, the Catalan Vengeance did not flag. Bands of Almugavars roamed at will through Thrace; a larger party, including many children of Almugavars receiving their first lesson in frightfulness, captured Rodosto and avenged horribly the brutal murder of their embassy. Where the citizens had quartered twenty-seven Catalans alive the new conquerors wreaked total revenge: men, women, children and animals were hacked in pieces, so that the Catalans could boast that no living being survived their passing. Wherever they went they left a similar trail of destruction; farmsteads were burned, livestock slaughtered or driven away and even the vines were torn out of the ground.

The town of Gallipoli was soon stocked to capacity with valuables and once more men of every nationality came, singly or in groups, to join the Company. Bands of Turkish and Turcopole mercenaries saw better chances of gain under the pales of Aragón than from the depreciated currency of Byzantium and a whole contingent of 2,000 crossed over from Anatolia for the same purpose. The Company has been unjustly accused of introducing Turks into Europe and hence of starting the train of events that led to the loss of Byzantium and the Balkans. Actually, the first mention of Turkish mercenaries being employed in Europe is in 1259, about half a century earlier, at the battle of Pelagonia, the first defeat suffered by the Frankish chivalry.[9] From then on it became the accepted thing to have a contingent of a thousand or two Turkish mercenaries, who fought well, grumbled little and were on the whole better behaved than the Greeks or Franks.

Now the Catalan merchants showed their worth and Gallipoli became a vast warehouse, crammed with goods for exchange or sale. Not the least valuable were the Greek captives, to whom a tariff of prices applied. Compared with a war horse at twenty-eight *perpres* and a pack-horse at fourteen, a male servant fetched only seven; but presumably supply and demand were the determining factors and the prospect of more peaceful times would cause a boom in Greek slaves. A flourishing trade arose with the Genoese and ancient enmities were forgotten as the Italian merchants bought girls and boys at knock-down prices for resale at a profit; the ultimate buyers were the rulers of Syria and Egypt, in whose establishments the merchandise would pass their lives as concubines, minions or eunuchs. A hundred years later Gallipoli, burned and rebuilt, was still a centre for the trade. Says Piloti the Venetian, 'There are in parts of Turkey and at the court of the Grand Turk, as at Adrianople and Gallipoli, several great heathen merchants who deal in no other merchandise than little male and female slaves of the right age to suit the Sultan and to be brought to Cairo . . . When they have one or two hundred souls, they take them to Gallipoli and put them on shipboard.'[10]

Among the riff-raff who flocked to the Catalan headquarters in the hope of sharing their spoils, and sometimes even their glory, one noble figure stands out. Ferdinand Jiménez d'Arenós, who left the Company at Cyzicus in 1303, had taken service with the Duke of Athens, gaining reputation and wealth during the wars of the duke with his Frankish neighbours. Now he felt the call of his reduced and besieged countrymen; whatever may have been the cause of his leaving the Company he bore them no ill-will and it is likely that his quarrel was a purely personal one with Roger de Flor. His employer in Athens was sympathetic to his loyalty and lent him a galley, so that he was able to reinforce the Catalans, amid universal rejoicing, with eighty veterans. He gained his footing quickly, for his first action was to call for volunteers and, with a force of 370, raid, massacre and burn up to the outskirts of Constantinople. The Emperor had to watch the havoc without being able to oppose the raiders, for the Turcopoles and Alani who were left in the city assumed that such boldness could only denote the presence of the Grand Company itself and refused to venture out against it. Once the truth became apparent he dispatched 2,800 men with orders to cut off the retreat of the raiding party at the River Batinia, where no alternative route was available. Need I recount the details? Once more the smaller, better disciplined and more ferocious force prevailed, killing three times their number of the enemy. By now the countryside was becoming so devastated that the Catalans had to divide their forces in order to forage successfully. The eastern part of Thrace was being ravaged by Bernard de Rocafort and the bulk of the Company, who had made their camp near Rodosto; Jiménez therefore besieged and captured Madytos, which lies near the tip of the Gallipoli peninsula, and made it his headquarters.

The year 1305 had indeed seen dramatic changes of fortune. The conquerors of Asia Minor suddenly became a persecuted, leaderless minority, with every man's hand against them. They lost their second leader by Genoese treachery and their Asian booty too, by another traitor. When their fortunes were at lowest ebb they destroyed their only means of retreat and went forth against incredible odds, perfectly confident in their own superiority and, perhaps with less reason, in the justice of their cause. The Catalan raiders now became bolder every day, some penetrating to Bizia (Vize) near the Black Sea Coast, others following the Aegean as far as Maronea, about thirty miles west of the present Greco-Turkish border. Each expedition left a swathe of ruined homesteads and the reek of putre-fying bodies.

At sea they were equally venturesome; the Sea of Marmara soon saw few vessels other than those of Catalan pirates and one expedi-tion excelled them all for sheer impertinence. By-passing Constan-tinople on foot they reached the Black Sea at Sthenia, the site of the imperial shipyards. Here they sacked and burned every ship with the exception of four, the galleys in which Ferdinand d'Aonés had brought Maria and her family back to Constantinople. After the massacre in Constantinople and the death of Aonés, his galleys, still laden with booty, were taken round to Sthenia for safe keeping. The Catalans, glad to be spared the homeward march through country they had already devastated, made all ship-shape and then rowed down the Bosphorus in their four galleys, and on its swift current passed under the astonished gaze of Byzantines and Genoese.

The Catalan Company ended the year with increased numbers, richer and stronger, masters of the Byzantine empire, with the ex-ception of the larger fortified cities. If a Greek ventured out of Constantinople or Adrianople he went in peril of his life. Even the parts they had not yet touched sensed their impending approach and Macedonia, to give an example, lay in pious expectation of the worst; they could expect no military help from their emperors, nor could they send their produce through desolate Thrace to its accus-tomed markets. The Genoese, too, had for the moment exchanged their enmity for the material advantages of slave trading in partner-ship. But the Catalans were not ready to rest on their laurels; they had scarcely begun to exact their vengeance.

Chapter 7

More deadly than the male
1306

The Thracian Chersonese, or Gallipoli peninsula, was now securely held, ready to declare itself part of the overseas territory of any of the branches of the royal house of Aragon. These were cautious, however, as long as the Company was homeless and friendless but, as we shall see, readier to act as patrons when better times arrived. Meanwhile the scorched earth policy was pursued, ever further afield, and in a short time the new desert would force the Catalans to move on. Records of serious opposition are lacking; only once does Muntaner tell us of a Greek raid, that of a certain Baron George of Christopolis.

While on his way to Constantinople this Thracian noble had the idea of raiding into the peninsula with eighty horsemen, taking advantage of the absence of most of the Company on marauding expeditions. Muntaner, governor of Gallipoli, used to send a small wagon train out every day to gather wood in the ravaged surroundings, under the command of one of his squires, a mounted archer named Marco. When he saw the raiding party approaching Marco ordered his four wood-gatherers to occupy a ruined tower and defend themselves with stones as best they could while he, Marco, galloped back to Gallipoli for help.[1] As it chanced, there were only six chargers and eight pack-horses to be found, so with these and such foot soldiers as could be got together Muntaner set out to the rescue. They did not have far to go: the eighty Greeks, having taken the wagons without opposition, had followed hard on Marco's heels and actually penetrated the outer defences of Gallipoli. 'And so,' wrote the chronicler, 'as we had done in other battles, we made to attack them all together, horse and foot; and thus it pleased our Lord, the true God,* that we defeated them and took thirty-seven horsemen, some dead, some captured, and we pursued the rest to the tower where my four men were on guard who had been with the wagon train, and then we let the rest go to perdition and returned to Gallipoli.' On the next day the captured horses and men were sold at the prices mentioned in the previous chapter and the proceeds divided among the handful of victorious Catalans. 'And I have told you of this pretty encounter, that you should each know that there is nothing greater than the power of God, and that it was not performed by our excellence, but by the goodness and grace of God.'

Now that their headquarters were presumed secure the Catalans felt they could venture further afield in their pursuit of revenge. The only enemies who had not felt the weight of their vengeance were the very ones who had murdered Roger and his officers, Gircon and the Alani. They had completed their contract and, so the Company was informed, were making their leisurely way to the steppes, across which they had to travel to their home in Circassia. Rocafort and Jiménez mustered every available man and set out in pursuit, leaving Muntaner in charge of Gallipoli. The camps at Rodosto (Tekirdag) and Madytos were closed and their non-combatants brought in to headquarters, which had been assigned 200 fighting men as a garrison. Their share of the booty had been promised them but nevertheless, during the night that followed the departure of the army, the majority disappeared in order to join the raid. Revenge or booty? The result was that Muntaner was left with seven armed horsemen and 133 infantry, partly Almugavars, partly sailors; 'poorly provided with men', he comments, 'but well found with women'.

Twelve full days' march were needed to catch up with the Alani, who had been warned that the Catalan Vengeance was pursuing them. On a plain at the foot of Mt Hemos, which then marked the border of Bulgaria though now it is well within that country, lay the camp. The Catalans had overtaken their prey only just in time, for it would have been beyond their powers to enter Bulgaria and fight that nation as well as their other enemies. After a night's rest the pursuers mustered outside the barricade of wagons that protected the camp of the Alani. These, with more valour than judgment,

* Not of course to be confused with the deity of the schismatic Greeks.

sallied out of their camp to do battle, the first 1,000 headed by Gircon and riding against the Company's cavalry. The battle was long and fierce, the Spaniards attempting time and again to penetrate inside the barricade, the Alani sallying forth to beat them back; insatiable thirst for vengeance urged on the one party, desperation, for their families if not for themselves, animated the other. The cavalry of both sides saw their formations shattered, their chargers killed and their weapons broken; still they fought, with teeth and bare hands, in a confused mass that reeled across the plain. Never had the Company been matched with so valiant an enemy, and from early morning till noon the issue remained in doubt. Then Gircon fell and as his head rolled the survivors thought to enter the barricade and defend their families and themselves from the shelter of the wagons. But a spearhead of Almugavars pressed through the gap along with the Alani. This by no means ended the battle, for they now found themselves faced by the wives and mothers of the enemy, in no way inferior in resolution to their menfolk. Another intensive struggle developed, as more Catalans found their way into the *laager*; but gradually their increasing numbers prevailed ove the diminishing defenders, now fighting in scattered groups.

When it became plain that all was lost, the Alani tried to save their women and children by mounting them on such few horses as survived; these, exhausted by the battle and in many cases wounded, could only stumble away with their double loads, so that the pursuers had little difficulty in overtaking them. The men turned in a last desperate stand, to give their wives more time to flee, and were cut down where they stood. Thus, in the whole of this bloody encounter scarcely 300 of the 9,000 Alani warriors escaped with their lives. Their heroic conduct in defeat must arouse a reluctant admiration, reluctant because these were the men who had massacred Roger and his unarmed companions at the dinner table.

A single episode, related by Muntaner,[2] illustrates the inflexible spirit of the Alani in adversity. He tells how a young Alan got his wife away from the lost battle; seeing three Catalans in pursuit and realizing that his own horses were weakening, he stopped, dismounted, embraced and kissed his wife before almost severing her head with a stroke of his sword. Then he turned on the pursuers; all three (Muntaner gives their names) were well mounted and were competent fighters. One was killed with a sword stroke that took off his left arm and the other two wounded before they slew him, a performance which was sure to arouse the admiration of the Almugavars, whose own creed was to fight grimly to the death.

When the tired victors could rest they found themselves masters of 400 wagons crammed with booty and hundreds of red-haired, blue-eyed girls and women; the luckier ones would become the concubines of the men who had slain their fathers and husbands and the rest would be sent to the slave market. The description of the women may give us the clue as to who the Alani were. They had, of course, nothing to do with the Alani who, in company with the Suevi, Vandals and other Germanic tribes, overran Europe nearly 1,000 years earlier. They are usually referred to as 'Alans of the Caucasus' and their sparse history includes the baptism of their king in the tenth century. I believe that they were Circassian Celts, one of the groups that retired into the mountainous regions before the next wave of invaders. Other groups of Celts survived in Asia Minor and among them were the Galatians; the sculptured group of these in the Museo delle Terme in Rome is nothing else than a demonstration of the scene described in the last paragraph. The defeated Galatian has just stabbed his wife and, supporting her body with his left arm, is preparing to kill himself. To the Celtic colouring of the females, therefore, must be added their choice of death rather than captivity.

Once the loot had been collected there was nothing to keep the Catalans away from home any longer. On the morrow the triumphal procession began to make its leisurely way south. Immense flocks of sheep, that had no doubt retarded the Alani in their journey north and enabled the avengers to overtake them, were driven back towards Gallipoli by the jubilant victors. Flushed with success they even tried to capture Adrianople and at least recover Roger's body, but their inability to prosecute a successful siege was once more demonstrated here, as at nearby Pamphylia. But even before they had attempted the assault, messengers arrived from Gallipoli with grave news.

It happened that a famous Genoese admiral, Antonio Spinola, was in Constantinople on matrimonial business. He had come to fetch Theodore Palaeologos, the second son of Andronicus' second marriage (see page 18), to marry his, Spinola's daughter in Genoa. Theodore's mother, Yolande or Irene[3] was Marchioness of Montferrat and had ceded the title to her son; the far-seeing Genoese was

Plate 1 Entry into Constantinople of Roger de Flor and
the Catalan Company, 1302

Plate 2 Bernat Desclot, first
Catalan chronicler

Plate 3 Death of Roger
de Flor

already tasting the fruits of a commercial as well as a matrimonial alliance with the Byzantine empire and the largest landowner in Greece, descendant of the Crusading leader of 1204. It was not like Andronicus to part too easily with such a gold-mine and he was considering the conditions he could impose. At that moment news arrived of the expedition against the Alani and the poorly defended state of Gallipoli. Here, at one blow, he might wipe out all the vexation that the Catalan Company had caused him. For once the time was ripe and the weapons to hand. Spinola had eighteen galleys of his own; his compatriot, Andrea Moresco, commanded seven other Genoese warships which, as we have heard, served at this time in the role of a Byzantine navy. This was the opportunity to destroy the robbers' lair, help themselves to the accumulated loot and leave the absent Catalan fighting men without a base.

Nothing seemed easier. In order to give an air of legality to the projected seizure, Spinola himself came to Gallipoli with two galleys and presented an ultimatum. The Catalans were to move out of their 'garden' forthwith, for it was a part of the Roman empire and reserved for the Genoese. If they refused, he added, they would be at war with, not only Byzantium, but Genoa and the Genoese, wherever they happened to be. Muntaner was an educated man; he pointed out that the Republic of Genoa was at peace with Aragón, Sicily and Mallorca and thus there was no justification for the issuing of an ultimatum, nor for its acceptance.[4] He may have added that Genoa's imprisonment of Entenza was itself unjustified. Twice more did Spinola issue a challenge and finally Muntaner answered that he would uphold the true faith of His Holiness the Pope, whose banner flew over the castle of Gallipoli, against the schismatic emperor and *all* his allies. Muntaner agreed readily to Spinola's demand that the challenge and reply be put on parchment and openly displayed. If the Genoese thought this would dishearten the meagre garrison he was mistaken; the Catalan showed no apprehension and behaved throughout as though Gallipoli was adequately defended. He announced solemnly that Spinola would be guilty of all damage and bloodshed arising from an unprovoked attack and that events would show the difference between words and deeds (Muntaner, ch. 227):

And one Saturday evening all the twenty-five galleys arrived before Gallipoli. And the whole of the day and the night they prepared ladders and engines for the siege, knowing that our Company was far away and that we were but few. And just as they were ordering their battle for the morrow, so I was ordering the defence all night; and the defence was so, that I had them arm all the women there were, for of weapons there were aplenty, and I stationed them on the walls, and to each section of the wall I sent a merchant of the Catalan merchants that there were, to be in command of the women.

He knew that the assault would be long and unremitting and that none would be able to go to their homes to eat, so bread and water and wine were set out in the streets where they could readily be obtained. All the defenders were ordered to wear helmets and cuirasses, as he knew that the Genoese would use crossbows; it was their custom, in fact, to discharge more bolts in one battle than the Catalans in ten.* Then, with his handful of mounted men he patrolled the shore, preventing the landing of besiegers from the galleys, until ten shiploads were disembarked farther up the coast and came upon him from the landward side.

Muntaner's horse was killed and he was defending himself on foot when one of his squires rode up and the two managed to get away on one horse, though Muntaner had by this time sustained five wounds. When the Genoese saw his charger fall they raised a shout, 'The captain's dead! At them! At them!', and when Muntaner rode back into the city, covered with his own blood and that of others, all thought he was dying; but he writes that the five wounds caused him little inconvenience, either in the administration of the defence or in the hand-to-hand fighting that followed. Now the Genoese were masters of the plain and pressed their assault, with all the more confidence when they saw that their opponents were but women. They soon found that what were women in the anatomical sense were invincible men in strength and determination. Thrown back from the walls with many dead and wounded at the first assault, they hoped that the natural weakness of the female would render the defenders unable to sustain a contest of endurance. But how they were mistaken! Again and yet again they were hurled back with even greater losses; some of the women threw down the scaling ladders with their bare hands while others engaged those who had

---

* It was the Genoese crossbowmen who so hampered their employers, the chivalry of France, at the battle of Crecy.

gained a foothold with sword and spear, their spirit rising even as the danger grew. The wounded fought on with the rest and one, with five wounds in her face, refused to leave the wall, protesting that the honour of fighting in her husband's place was not to be surrendered, except with her life.

But the Genoese would not retire. As one man fell from the scaling ladders another took his place. By now the crossbowmen had run out of ammunition, the wounded outnumbered the hale, and the fierce July sun beat down on the dusty field and the exhausted assailants. Seeing from his flagship that the attack was faltering, Spinola decided to intervene. Landing with 400 horsemen he rode up to the walls, intent on heartening the attackers. At the head of his armoured knights, from whose glittering array rose five banners, he drew up before the Iron Gate and cursed his men for allowing scurvy rabble to sustain a defence.[15] Another assault was ordered.

Now followed an episode which makes the previous deeds appear but commonplace. Muntaner came down from the wall and had all six—six, mark you—of the Company's chargers saddled, then he called 100 of his infantry and bade them discard their defensive armour, for bolts and arrows were used up and the sun was fierce. With his five fresh wounds he mounted, mustered his men within the gate and commended their cause to God and the Blessed Virgin. The gate was thrown open and 'with the six armoured horsemen and the foot that were now so light, we hurled ourselves at the banners so that we had four of them down at the first shock . . . What shall I tell you? That Antonio lost his head [literally] in the very place where he had delivered his challenges, and with him the gentles who accompanied him, so that more than six hundred Genoese died here.' The chronicler now reports a great disappointment, for having chased the fugitives to the shore they were confronted by 100 fresh Genoese and, themselves weary and worn, were obliged to let the others escape.

But when news was brought that the famous Antonio Boccanegra was holding out on a hill-top with forty men, they found strength to attack him too. Valiantly he resisted, until all his companions had been killed or taken; then Muntaner, as courteous as he was brave, implored him to surrender. Sternly the Genoese refused and the Catalans, angered at his arrogant bearing, threw themselves upon him and bore him down to earth by sheer weight of numbers, rapidly dispatching him. Spinola's galleys went on to Genoa with the Count of Montferrat, leaving his future father-in-law dead on the field; the others returned to Constantinople.

News of the Genoese attack had meanwhile reached the main body of the Catalans, who were now outside Adrianople. The siege, such as it was, was abandoned and the troops pressed on by forced marches, afraid that they would arrive too late to relieve Gallipoli. But they had no need to fear. The Catalan Company had written a fresh page in the annals of war. No atrocity, no dissension, no future perfidy would dim the glory of that day.

The Company had not forgotten Muntaner's promise to Berenguer d'Entenza and had continued to petition the rulers of Catalonia, Sicily and Mallorca, all members of the House of Aragón, for their help in securing his release. It was James II of Aragón (which included Catalonia) who succeeded in persuading the Genoese that Entenza was a member of a nation with whom they were not at war, and that his detention was unjustified. A document from Naples shows that he was at liberty on 29 January 1306. The Company's envoys had reinforced their plea by offering James the territory they had conquered in the east, but the king, who had enough hay on his fork, as the saying goes, declined; he suggested politely that the offer might be of more interest to his brother Frederick of Sicily, who, in any case, was nearer the scene. We shall see what came of this. The attempt to secure restitution for Entenza's material losses was less successful; embassies went to and fro, excuses were offered and counter-claims made. He was given his liberty and nothing more.

It is understandable that Entenza did not wish to rejoin the Company without the following that he considered suitable for his rank and breeding. He made representations to the Pope, and then to the King of France, asking for their aid in the Catalan Company's war against the empire of Byzantium. Strangely enough, neither ruler would promise help, although the restoration of Latin rule in Constantinople was one of their avowed aims. Perhaps they had yet to learn that the modest numbers of the Catalans bore no relation to their capacity for conquest. Entenza had therefore to rely on his own resources. The head of the junior, Catalan branch of a noble Aragonese family, he had left home at an early age in order to take part in the Sicilian war. Since then he had scarcely seen his home and before recruiting a new contingent he had to ascertain what he could realize of the family fortune. Between purchaser and pawn-broker he disposed of a large part of his land and used the proceeds to hire a ship from a certain Peter Solivera[6] of Barcelona. At the same time he recruited 500 men-at-arms and sailed with these to Gallipoli, where Muntaner received him with respect and honour. But not so Rocafort. We witnessed the resentment of the self-made man for the aristocrat before Entenza's ill-fated expedition; his enmity had not abated during their separation. Moncada sums up their incompatibility: the one, he says, was an aristocrat, courteous, liberal and suave; the other a simple gentleman, rough, jealous and arrogant.

Entenza naturally expected to resume his position as commander-in-chief, to which post Roger had appointed him on his departure to the fatal meeting at Adrianople. Rocafort vehemently opposed the pretension and the undignified wrangle almost culminated in blows. In Entenza's favour it was urged that he had been taken prisoner by Genoese treachery and not through any fault of his own; that he had suffered imprisonment because he was their leader, and not for any private transgression; that he had been robbed of his possessions; that he had sold much of his private estate in order to bring them reinforcements; and finally, added his rash supporters, there was the difference in birth to consider.

The last argument only added fury to the passionate claims of Rocafort's friends. They reminded the Council of Entenza's ill-advised expedition, his autocratic behaviour, his overruling of the Council's recommendations, and of the parlous situation in which they were left when Entenza was captured. In contrast, they urged (Moncada, ch. 47):

Rocafort has been our commander for years! [It was, in fact, just over a year.] He took over when we were almost without hope, our cause as good as lost, and by his own exertions restored us to the position of one of the most feared and respected nations of the east. It would be unjust to take away his command at the peak of success, when he has retained it through the most critical times. Let him have the fruit of the toil, who carried it to success! It would be shameful if the others, however great and noble, were to take from him the post in which Rocafort has gained such renown and so many notable victories, saving us from a miserable death.

Muntaner and the twelve councillors tried to compose the dispute, hoping that the parties would behave once more as brothers in arms. All their tact was needed, as voices became louder and threats began to take the place of argument. More than once the leaders and their supporters made to draw on each other. In the end the only arrangement that suited all parties was that Entenza should make his forays with such as volunteered to accompany him, and Rocafort should do the same. At this juncture Jiménez d'Arenós, another aristocrat, declared that he too preferred independence—not for the first time, you will remember—and there were thus three parties, not counting the pacific Muntaner. Quite understandably, the majority elected to follow Rocafort; his daring had led them almost to the walls of Constantinople; his reputation was such that the Tsar of Bulgaria, Theodore Sventislas, had offered him an alliance and the hand of his sister, the widowed daughter-in-law of the emperor of the Tartars. To the Turkish contingent Rocafort was the commander who had employed them and with primitive loyalty they refused to recognize another.

In this way, thanks to the efforts of Muntaner and the Council, the first rift in the Company appeared to be settled, if not amicably at least without bloodshed. Though outwardly satisfied, each leader felt inwardly that he had been cheated and looked forward to the day when he could erase the affront to his dignity. The only hopeful development was the decision of Jiménez to join forces with Entenza, his social equal. If we are to believe Pachymeres, he had already been negotiating secretly with Andronicus, with a view to bringing his eighty men to take service with the Byzantines.[7] But for the time being the combined strength of Entenza and Jiménez, though not nearly equalling that of Rocafort, would at least make them a factor which the other could not ignore. There remained unmistakable tension between the groups and Muntaner, who had remained neutral throughout, heaved a sigh of relief when the several armies of Rocafort and Entenza left Gallipoli on their next raid. The former, with the Almugavars and Turks, took the coast road of Thrace and laid siege to Nona (Aenus, Enez); the latter followed for half of the way and blockaded the castle of Megarix, on the gulf of Saros. His followers included all the Aragonese and such others as had claims to gentle birth, as well as a detachment of Catalan sailors.

At about this time there occurred an incident which, trivial in itself, indicated the high repute gained by the Catalans as fighters and—note this—as men of honour. A certain Ticino Zaccaria, member of a leading Genoese family, came to the Catalans with his eighty-oared galley; his object was to enlist their aid in recovering from an uncle what he considered should by rights be his own castle. The rights or wrongs of his grievance are irrelevant to our tale. The first point of interest is that a Genoese should come trustingly to the Catalans, asking for help and offering to serve them faithfully in return;[8] the second is that Ticino is fraudulently inscribed in the Company's payroll and ration book as being accompanied by ten armed knights. This, it is naïvely explained, was a common practice, by which friends or favourites could draw more than their entitlement from the quartermaster. A time-honoured, universal and persistent dodge.

A raiding force was quickly assembled under the leadership of Muntaner's cousin John and sent off in five vessels. They sailed on the day after Palm Sunday and arrived at New Phocaea[9] on the night of Easter Sunday. By dawn of the next day a small party had scaled the castle wall before the sentries were alerted, gates were flung open and, amid the usual scenes of carnage, New Phocaea fell to the combined Genoese and Catalans. Being a source of alum (used as a mordant in dyeing, as well as in tanning and in the paper industry) New Phocaea was a wealthy trading post and when the loot came up for division the raiders were not disappointed. Among the most valuable of the treasures was the customary, but still almost priceless, piece of the True Cross, to wit, from the part against which the Saviour had rested his head;[10] St John the Evangelist had been in the habit of wearing it suspended round his neck. There was a vestment of the same evangelist, allegedly worked by the hand of the Blessed Virgin herself and, as the *pièce de résistance*, an autographed copy of the Book of Revelation. All three relics were said to have been placed on the altar of the basilica at Ephesus (Selçuk) by St John himself. When the town fell to the Seljuks the holy objects disappeared along with other more readily convertible prizes. But they were not destined to remain for ever in pagan hands; the most marvellous part of the story is that the priceless relics had been pawned to Ticino's uncle Benito by the Turks, as security for a consignment of wheat.[11]

Chapter 8

The fatal quarrel
1307

Bernard de Rocafort was brilliant, bold and a born leader. He was what was called a private gentleman and his choice of a career shows that he was neither prosperous nor of aristocratic descent; this helps to explain the events of the next two years. Nowhere was social standing so rigidly defined as in Spain; the gulf that separated royalty from the grandees, who were allowed to keep on their headgear in the monarch's presence, was offset by that between the grandee and the *ricohombre*, while the *ricohombre* was far and away superior to the *hidalgo* (the *hijo de algo*, or Son of Something). Rocafort fell into the last category, possibly as the younger son of a younger son, and like many able men resented the advantages of aristocracy over achievement. For he had come a long way from his modest origin, so humble indeed that one author makes him rise from the ranks of the Almugavars.[1] With brain and sword and resolution he had carved out a career until now he was undisputed head of an army, almost of a nation. In the spring of 1307 his rise to greater heights was suddenly threatened from an unexpected quarter.

On 10 March a pact was signed at Milazzo between Frederick II of Sicily and his first cousin, Prince Ferdinand (see pp. 96–7). The latter was a younger son of James, King of Mallorca, and both were grandsons of the great James the Conqueror, of Aragón. Frederick, who had so often been begged for positive support of the Company, had always put off their embassies with fair words and procrastination. He had even evaded intervening on behalf of Berenguer d'Entenza, whose release was finally obtained by Frederick's elder brother, James II of Aragón. But that was when the Catalan Company was outnumbered, friendless and far from home; with the rise in their fortunes Frederick's caution was partly relaxed. Not sufficiently, mark you, to commit him to the role of active participant, but enough to enable him to share their success. By the pact's terms, therefore, Ferdinand would join the Company as its commander-in-chief, and fealty would be sworn to him *as his cousin's representative*. Thus Frederick stood to gain a new colony while his cousin, the dashing Ferdinand, took the risks. It did not occur to the brave and brainless prince that Frederick had waited at least four years before accepting the loyal duty of the adventurers. This was caution indeed, for as early as 1304 Frederick had sent a message, by Admiral Roger de Lluria, to his brother James II. The letter has survived and it clearly states Frederick's intention of conquering Byzantium.[2]

Ferdinand arrived at Gallipoli and was warmly welcomed by Muntaner. The prince was the first volunteer of royal blood (we may forget Sancho Pere) to join the Company and the chronicler furthermore had a special feeling of loyalty, for his ancestors had accompanied the first James in the conquest of Mallorca; the name still survives in the Balearic Islands, where both a Montaner and a Muntaner maintain the gifts of the old quartermaster in the guise of hotel proprietors. The few men who had remained at Gallipoli made no difficulty about accepting the new arrival as Frederick's representative. Couriers were sent to Entenza, Rocafort and Jiménez d'Arenós, giving news of the prince's arrival and Frederick's letters confirming his function of delegate. Meanwhile Muntaner, whom we might call the only gentleman (as distinct from nobleman) in the Company, gave up his lodging—the best in town—and put fifty horses and a greater number of mules at Ferdinand's disposal.

The first to arrive was Entenza, who hurried back from the siege of Megarix with a handful of companions, welcomed the prince and swore the required oath of fealty. Next came Jiménez from Madytos, equally agreeable. In fact, 'we all had great joy and held our cause to be won, since God had brought us the aforesaid Lord Prince, who was of the direct line of Aragón, as he was son of the Lord King of Mallorca; and further, that he was one of the first four cavaliers of the world, both in person and in wisdom, and strove greatly to give

Table 3

Kings of Sicily and Mallorca from 1282

(Rulers in capital letters and their dates refer to their reign in Sicily only)

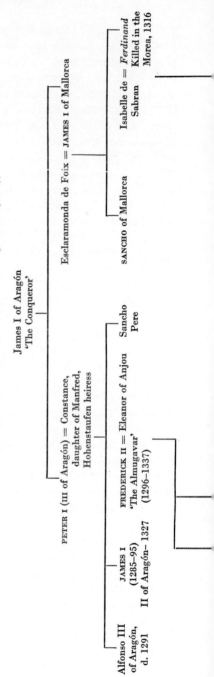

James I of Aragón
'The Conqueror'

PETER I (III of Aragón) = Constance, daughter of Manfred, Hohenstaufen heiress

Esclaramonda de Foix = JAMES I of Mallorca

Alfonso III of Aragón, d. 1291

JAMES I (1285–95) II of Aragón– 1327

FREDERICK II = Eleanor of Anjou 'The Almugavar' (1296–1337)

Sancho Pere

SANCHO of Mallorca

Isabelle de = Ferdinand Sabran Killed in the Morea, 1316

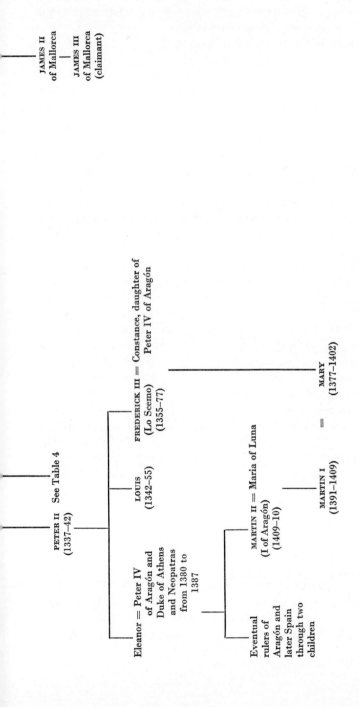

JAMES II
of Mallorca

JAMES III
of Mallorca
(claimant)

PETER II
(1337–42)

See Table 4

Eleanor = Peter IV
of Aragón and
Duke of Athens
and Neopatras
from 1380 to
1387

LOUIS
(1342–55)

FREDERICK III = Constance, daughter of
(Lo Scemo)   Peter IV of Aragón
(1355–77)

MARTIN II = Maria of Luna
(I of Aragón)
(1409–10)

Eventual
rulers of
Aragón and
later Spain
through two
children

MARTIN I
(1391–1409)

=

MARY
(1377–1402)

true justice; so that, for many reasons, he had come at the right moment'. So, at least, thought Muntaner.

To Rocafort the moment was anything but opportune. Scarcely had he shown his independence of Entenza, and indirectly of the power of the nobility, when royalty itself arrived. His old arguments, even his popularity with the Almugavars and Turks, were useless in the new circumstances. To add to his problems, his men had received the news of the prince's arrival with joy, and there was thus no apparent possibility of successfully precipitating an open rupture. Rocafort's aim at this stage was an ambitious one, no less than to have the Company choose him as leader over the head of the prince.

His first care was therefore to make sure that he would be surrounded by his own supporters, and that his rivals would be absent, when the confrontation took place. He accordingly sent a message to Gallipoli, extending his welcome and expressing his own and his men's great pleasure at the prince's arrival; he begged to be excused from attending him personally and as promptly as he would have liked, but that the siege of Nona was now well advanced and his presence at its final stages essential. Hence Ferdinand was invited most cordially to come to Nona, where he was eagerly awaited.

Rocafort's reply had the desired effect. Ferdinand took counsel with his aristocratic vassals, whom he would have liked to take with him, and asked if it was essential that he join Rocafort immediately. Unfortunately all were of one mind, that he should go to Nona as soon as possible, before the joyful news of his arrival had time to become stale among Rocafort's men. And, with regard to their accompanying him, they were convinced that Rocafort was more likely to swear fealty if the prince was not accompanied by his noble friends. It would be better for all if they followed him and arrived when Rocafort had taken the oath and they were all on an equal footing. First round to Rocafort, who was as superior in craftiness as he was skilled in arms.

His next step was to hold a meeting of the Council, at which he instilled an idea that was as effective as a draught of poison: while they had the greatest affection and loyalty for the prince and, indeed, all the royal house of Aragón, they felt that King Frederick of Sicily had been somewhat tardy in acceding to their frequent prayers for recognition. They would welcome Ferdinand and would willingly take the oath of fealty—but to him, in his own right, and not to his cousin Frederick. Well did Rocafort gauge the loyal Ferdinand's reaction.

The prince duly arrived after a three days' journey and was received with appropriate expressions of satisfaction on the part of all. He was feasted for several days, but the questions of submission and the oath of fealty to his cousin were somehow evaded. At length he asked Rocafort to summon a meeting of the Council, to hear the substance of the letters which he was carrying for the King of Sicily, and Rocafort, whose poison had now been spreading through the camp for several days, showed his great pleasure in obeying. The Council on this occasion was the general one, consisting of every soldier on the payroll, and not solely the executive.

The prince appeared before them with his entourage and bade a secretary read aloud the substance of the royal letter. The king, moved by their prayers, had accepted their embassies' oaths of fidelity; although the circumstances of his own kingdom made it impossible for him to undertake their defence, he nevertheless wished to demonstrate to them the love that he entertained and consequently had sent his cousin to govern them in his name and offered even greater support—in the future. The spokesman for the Company replied, as prearranged, that they would take counsel together and then give their answer.

Rocafort stayed on during their deliberations, for there was obviously no unanimity; the meeting, in fact, included officers who seemed likely to welcome Ferdinand as their chief, even in his role as deputy for the King of Sicily, Rocafort suggested that a council of this size could not deliberate the minutiae which were so important and that they should elect a committee of fifty, who would report back to them, so that they could all accept or reject their recommendations. He knew all about crowd psychology—at least Moncada credits him with knowing that, if the mob believes in a person, it will continue to do so, without bothering about the merits of his counsel.[3] As regards the fifty, the majority were his creatures already and the rest were prepared to believe what he chose to tell them. Though they were sworn to secrecy, his speech is reported in full by Muntaner (ch. 230), who probably used the licence which historians, from Herodotus onwards, have employed.

Men! God has shown us great love in sending this lord among us, for in the whole world there is none who can be of greater

merit. This one is of the direct line of the House of Aragón
and is one of the foremost cavaliers of the world, and is of
those who love truth and justice. Wherefore I would advise
that one and all, we receive him as commander. But he has
told us that we should accept him on behalf of the Lord King
of Sicily. This we should by no means do, for it is of much
greater profit to us that he should be our commander, than
the King of Sicily; for Ferdinand has no lands over which to
rule, so that he will always be with us and we with him. That
King of Sicily—well, you know what reward he gave us for the
services we did him, us and our fathers; that as soon as peace
came, he threw us out of Sicily with a hundredweight of bread
apiece. That is something that each one of you should remember! So let us make answer that not for anything should we
receive him on behalf of King Frederick, but that we are
ready to accept him for his own sake, as the grandson of one
who was our natural lord,* held in great honour by us, and
that we are ready to give him fealty and homage; whereby he
will have great gain of us and we shall do our duty by him.
And we shall remind the King of Sicily that he remember what
he did to us when he made peace.

With these and many other specious arguments he roused them.
'Had the king offered his help when it was so sorely needed? No,
but only when it suited him and was of no service to us. And then,
at long last, did he send arms, fighting men, supplies or money to
carry on a war? No, only a general and commander to govern us,
who need no other leader.' For fifteen days the matter was debated,
while the siege of Nona was prosecuted, and the loyal Ferdinand
did precisely what Rocafort had counted on: he would, he told
them, stay as the representative of King Frederick or else return
immediately to Sicily. In order to avoid too abrupt a rupture,
Rocafort prevailed on him to accompany the army as far as Macedonia, which was their next objective.

The move was a forced one. Gallipoli had been ravaged so
thoroughly that no living thing survived within ten days' march in
any direction; Pachymeres adds that the stink of unburied men and
horses was in any case so great that the Company was forced to
leave.[4] Ferdinand arranged the march so that there would be the

---

* James the Conqueror.

least chance of conflict breaking out between the factions. Muntaner would take the Company's twenty-four vessels and convey women, children and stores, which included the treasure they had amassed. The army would take the coast road, now that both Megarix and Nona had fallen, Rocafort a day's march ahead of Entenza, Jiménez and the prince. They were all to meet at Christopolis, now Cavalla. The latter name was given to the city much later, when it was an important remount station for the postal service. St Paul landed there (Acts 16: 11) when it was still Neapolis, and its next name, Christopolis, is said to derive from his visit.

But a curse hung over the Company. 'With what measure ye mete, it shall be measured unto you' applies aptly. The rivers of blood they shed were by no means entirely at the expense of their enemies or of innocent civilians. Just two days' march short of Christopolis Rocafort's men crossed the River Nestos, which marked the limit of the ravaged territory of Thrace. Discipline was poor, for no enemy was near, and the sudden change to an abundance of food and, above all, fresh fruit was too much for them. Instead of leaving their camp with the dawn they stayed on all day, gorging themselves. By chance Berenguer d'Entenza, with the vanguard of his force, made an unusually rapid march and came on Rocafort's rearguard without warning. Then there happened the very tragedy that Ferdinand had tried to prevent. Each party thought the other was about to attack and a murderous struggle developed. Entenza, unarmed as he was, sprang to horse and spurred forward to separate the contestants and recall his men. Rocafort's brother Gisbert and his uncle Dalmau de San Martín thereupon rode against him with lances; Entenza had time only to turn in his saddle and ask, 'What is this, friends?', when they were upon him and an instant later he lay dead. Some say that the killing was to pay off old scores; others that there was a genuine mistake, the Rocafort party believing that Entenza, far from recalling his men, was urging them on to attack. Now Rocafort himself arrived and encouraged the Turks in his division to complete the work begun by the Almugavars.

Jiménez d'Arenós had also ridden forward unarmed, but when he saw what had happened to Entenza he turned away in disgust, called round him such of his troop as were within hail and rode away to a neighbouring castle. From there he went eastward, eventually presenting himself to Andronicus as a candidate for employment.

The Emperor accepted him and his men eagerly, conferred on him the now vacant title of Grand Duke and married him to a widowed niece. The imperial family may have been short of cash; they always had a supply of nubile females. There Jiménez leaves our tale, but remains on record as the only fighting leader (Muntaner counted as headquarters staff) to survive the hazards of the expedition. Roger de Flor was dead, and Aonés, Corberán, Entenza and how many more officers we cannot know; but the grim tally was still incomplete.

Near the scene of the tragedy there was a church with a chapel to St Nicholas in the crypt, and there they buried Berenguer d'Entenza and had masses said and put up a fine monument near the altar. 'May God keep his soul,' says Muntaner, 'for he was a true martyr, in that he died correcting the evil that we did.' So died the noblest of the few well-born captains of the expedition, far from his family home at Ribagorza. An ancestor was uncle to James the Conqueror and the great Admiral Lluria, who was also Berenguer's brother-in-law; a castle near Valencia bears the family name, recording faithful service to the king. His deeds, as well as his bearing, were worthy of his gentle birth.[5]

The murder of Entenza, for as such it was regarded by all but Rocafort's supporters, persuaded Prince Ferdinand to have his own position defined once and for all. His own four galleys arrived from Gallipoli at this time and he had the means for parting with Rocafort, whom by now he regarded with distrust. He therefore ordered the Company's Council to meet again and once more asked them whether they would receive him as commander in the name of his cousin Frederick, as otherwise he was resolved to leave. Rocafort's influence was stronger than ever and the Company's answer more emphatic, but unchanged. We have seen that it was not in the prince's nature to be disloyal to his cousin Frederick; he refused the leadership in his own name, embarked and made for the Island of Thasos, which lies only a few miles offshore from the scene of Entenza's death. Rocafort was left undisputed commander of the Catalan Company. Muntaner, with the non-combatants and supplies, arrived at the island at the same time and Ferdinand, after recounting the disgraceful facts of the brawl at the River Nestos, advised him to leave the expedition and accompany him to Sicily.

Now they profited by Muntaner's altruism in helping Ticino Zaccaria to regain his rights, while still at Gallipoli; for the same

Plate 4 The burning tower of Adrianople

Plate 5 Ramón Muntaner, soldier and chronicler, defender of Gallipoli

Genoese was now owner of Thasos, where he made the Prince and Muntaner welcome; he even offered the former the keys of his castle and undertook to serve him in any capacity. Thus, says Muntaner in moralizing mood and in medieval Catalan, does kindness pay off: '*Fes plaer, e no quarts aqui*', or, in proverbial rhyming Castilian:

> '*Haz bien*
> *Y no mires a quien.*'

Doing good, in this instance, meant lending killers to kill other killers.

Muntaner was relieved of much apprehension by Ferdinand's advice, for he shared every sensible man's distrust of a tyrant. Nevertheless it was his duty to complete his journey, deliver his passengers and give a reckoning of the valuables he carried for the men of the Company. He therefore sailed along the coast and found Rocafort a day's march west of the Nestos, where Entenza had been killed. Prudently, and very much in character, he allowed no one to disembark until he had been assured that no harm would come to the wives, children and property of Entenza and Jiménez d'Arenós.

The women were now offered the choice of joining Jiménez and his men, remaining with Rocafort or taking ship for the Venetian-held Negroponte, the long island off the east coast of the Greek mainland that today, as in classical times, is called Euboea. We are not told which offer they chose. Muntaner's departure was marked by another assembly of the Grand Council of the Company, at which he handed over the account books and the great seal. It would have been out of character if he had not made a farewell speech; it was expected of him, for we have ample evidence of his popularity and oratory has always been a welcome diversion of the illiterate. He told them that his orders to leave came from the Prince himself, whom he dare not disobey; that he had delayed in order to hand over his responsibilities; that his departure was solely the result of their behaviour and, sad though he was to leave them, it was they who had killed the noble Entenza and lost Jiménez, who had for their sakes relinquished his post at Athens (Muntaner, ch. 233).

> And they prayed me not to go from them, and above all the Turks and Turcopoles, who came to me weeping and begging that I would not abandon them, for they counted me as a

father to them, and indeed they used to call me *cata*, which in Turkish is to say 'father'. And in truth I felt greater sadness at leaving them than any others, for they had enlisted under my command and placed greater trust in me than in any other of the army of the Christians.

The further adventures of Prince Ferdinand of Mallorca and Ramón Muntaner are still bound up with the Company's fortunes. They also bring home to us the insecurity of prince and commoner in the old days. Summer was well advanced when the little fleet of six vessels left Thasos, heading south on the first leg of their journey to Sicily, where they would report the failure of the prince's mission. Immediately to the north of Negroponte is the beautiful bay of Volo and on its shores lay the town of Halmyros, at that time a centre of some importance. Here they arrived, Muntaner in the second best galley, the *Española*, graciously put at his disposal by his friend the prince. The latter had called at Halmyros on his way to Gallipoli and providently left four men with orders to make ship's biscuits for future eventualities. Now there was no sign of them and we cannot learn whether they died, were killed or taken away into captivity. Their disappearance reminds one of the garrison that Columbus left in Hispaniola during his first voyage, killed by the natives they had ill-treated before the admiral's return in 1493. It was obviously assumed by the prince that the worst had happened.

We do not even know whether Ferdinand made any enquiries before subjecting the town to another example of Catalan vengeance. His head was as weak as his heart was stout, otherwise he would surely have reflected that this part of Thessaly, Greater Vlachia, was not only nominally governed by the Greek John II Angelos, but was under the protection of the powerful Frankish lord, the second Guy de la Roche of Athens. The satisfaction with which Muntaner recorded that the missing men were well avenged, in that the whole town was consigned to the flames, was not to last, Ferdinand committed his next stupidity by sailing to the nearby island of Skopelos, which he ravaged thoroughly; though it may have been Byzantine territory, as he believed, the governor was a Venetian, Tiepolo-Ghisi, who could not be dislodged from his castle. Any other idiot would now have been satisfied, but Ferdinand was made of denser stuff. He recalled that he had been well received on his outward voyage by the Venetians who owned Negroponte and, against Muntaner's advice, decided to call there again on the way home. The ships therefore made their way down the Gulf of Euboea to the city of Negroponte (Chalkis), and anchored among Venetian men-of-war in a colony allied to the Duke of Athens, whose beard they had singed at Halmyros. Here Muntaner feelingly remarks how dangerous it is to travel with young sons of kings, who think that their royal blood will ensure their being treated with proper respect.[6] And so it ought to be, he adds, but it isn't.

To understand what happened next we have to turn back to an episode in the complicated international politics of the time. As I have mentioned earlier (Chapter 2), one of the claimants to the throne of Byzantium was Charles of Valois, known as 'the perpetual pretender', 'king of the hat and the wind', and other even less flattering titles. A brother of Philip the Fair, the French king who was even then getting ready to suppress the Templars with barbarous cruelty, Charles had first married a second cousin, Margaret the grand-daughter of Charles of Anjou, and then Catherine de Courtenay, heiress to the Latin emperors of Constantinople; it will be remembered that the last of these had run away before the threat of the Palaeologos restoration. Charles thus had a double, and doubly shadowy claim to the Byzantine empire. It had as much chance of success as the earlier, papally supported schemes of making him king of Aragon, and later king of Sicily. About a quarter of a century earlier he had made an agreement with the Venetians, with the object of recovering the Latin empire of Byzantium, but with more pressing engagements it had lapsed; in 1306, a year before this episode, Charles had sent an emissary, Thibaut de Cepoy, to renew the agreement.

In short then, Charles of Valois was a claimant to the throne of Byzantium; his envoy Thibaut de Cepoy had procured an alliance with the Venetians and was now on his way to Macedonia to visit Bernard de Rocafort. His object was to hire the Catalan Company to capture Constantinople for Charles.

The Venetian men-of-war, among which the prince and Muntaner now found themselves, were bringing Thibaut on this very mission. Charles of Valois had no love for the House of Aragón; this of course included Prince Ferdinand, and the Venetians, as well as being his allies, were still smarting under the sack of the island of Skopelos. It should therefore have caused no surprise, even to the feather-brained Ferdinand, that in spite of a solemn promise of safe conduct he was seized as soon as he stepped ashore at Negroponte; at the same time the Venetian warships attacked his unprepared vessels.

Muntaner reports that their principal target was the *Española*, which contained his personal treasure. He adds that more than forty of her complement were killed and he himself would doubtless have been singled out for murder except that he had determined not to move from the side of Prince Ferdinand. He thus became a captive along with the Prince and ten of his entourage, while his galley was emptied of everything of value that he possessed. As a careful campaigner Muntaner had amassed, in perfectly honest fashion, 25,000 ounces of gold, as well as valuable ornaments and clothes. All were stolen by the rapacious Venetians and, as we shall learn, were never returned, though his grand-daughter managed to get back a tenth part of the lost property some forty years later.[7]

After lodging for some days with Bonifacio da Verona, who was destined to play an important part in the Company's future, Ferdinand was sent under strong guard to Guy de la Roche, Duke of Athens; the latter was still resentful at the burning of Halmyros, which was supposed to be under his protection. The prince was imprisoned in the castle-palace of Thebes, known throughout the western world as the Castle of St Omer, a building whose beauties were one of the wonders of the age.[8] Its history is interesting: about half a century previously the lord of St Omer, to whom Thebes had passed by marriage to a de la Roche, built the castle of Cadmeia. It soon took the name of its owner, at least unofficially, and such is the tenacity of folk memory that the one remaining tower of the castles of Estives, or Thebes, is still called Santameri, after St Omer, by the inhabitants.[9]

Having thus neatly disposed of one commander of the Catalan Company, Thibaut de Cepoy devised means of ingratiating himself with its officers. He assumed that Muntaner's great treasure must have been gained dishonestly and that the chronicler was a fugitive embezzler; by returning him to the men he had robbed Thibaut thought to gain considerable credit, even though the gold itself could not be detached from the Venetian grasp. At the same time he would deliver another fugitive, García Gómez Palacín, a friend of Entenza and Jiménez, and thus a suspected enemy of Rocafort.

Sure enough, when Cepoy arrived in Cassandria, where he had arranged to meet Rocafort, the latter had Gómez Palacín summarily beheaded without trial or consultation, a foretaste of the autocratic bearing which was to develop into megalomania. But Muntaner's reception was very different and anything but satisfying to Thibaut. Rocafort embraced him and all the others crowded round, eager to kiss his hand. Moncada remarks on the rarity of such affection for headquarters staff, who were (and often still are) assumed to enrich themselves in safety while their comrades braved hardships and danger.[10] They gave him the best lodgings available and the Turks and Turcopoles began by presenting him with twenty horses and 1,000 gold *bezants*; Rocafort gave him a valuable charger, a mule, food and forage, and in fact there was no one of consequence in the army who did not press something on him. Thibaut and the Venetian captains stood aghast at these manifestations of affection and respect, fearing that Muntaner might turn the host against them by complaining of the treatment he had received. It is true that the Catalans knew of the theft of his effects, for he tells how they wept for him at his loss, but they were soon weeping again at the joy of seeing him back among them. Presents poured in on him and he estimates their value at 4,000 *bezants*. He did not allow his popularity to go to his head; his prudence can be judged from his reserved attitude. He did not accuse the Venetians of being personally responsible for his loss, nor did he demand instant satisfaction. Sensitive to atmosphere, he trusted neither the Venetians' sudden amiability nor Rocafort's. He had lived long enough with bloodthirsty, grasping, ambitious adventurers.

Perhaps this is not how he thought of them consciously, for Spanish writers have consistently portrayed the Company as the injured party. Even twenty years later, when Muntaner began to write his chronicle at the age of sixty, he enlists our sympathy for this band of ruffians. Cheated of their pay, their leaders treacherously murdered, even their ambassadors barbarously slaughtered, abandoned by their liege lords and with every man's hand against them, theirs was a struggle for bare survival. That, at least, is how their case is presented by their compatriots. The reader will by now have read enough to decide that neither Empire nor Company nor Franks were wholly innocent, or wholly to blame.

It was now that Rocafort had to make up his mind whether or not he should accept employment by Charles of Valois. On the one hand it would mean subordinating himself to a new chief, though he thought he could deal with that difficulty. Against this, he balanced the fact that the Company's refusal to accept Ferdinand would finally alienate the three branches of the House of Aragón which had, in any case, shown little enthusiasm for their cause. It must have been especially galling at a time when colonial territories and advantageous trade concessions could be had almost for the asking and were being exploited by the far-seeing Pisans, Venetians and Genoese.[11]

A further temptation lay in the funds which Thibaut had brought and would receive from Charles in the future: since its employment by the impoverished Palaeologi the Company had appreciated a sound paymaster. Again, Thibaut had by sheer chance captured Prince Ferdinand, representing an Aragonese employer; his star was in the ascendant. We may suspect—in fact we may be sure from certain facts that will be given later—that Rocafort had made up his mind when he once more summoned a meeting of the General Council of the Company. Their first resolution was to demand the return of Muntaner's stolen property; Thibaut and the Venetians were told that he had been 'their father and their governor' since they left Sicily and had to swear that restitution would be made.[12]

The next subject to be deliberated was the mission of Thibaut de Cepoy. Rocafort spoke strongly in favour of being employed by Charles of Valois under the same terms as they had accepted from Andronicus; the pay would therefore be four ounces of gold per month for an armoured horseman, two for light horse and one for a foot soldier. He pointed out that they had no further hope of recognition by Aragón, Sicily or Mallorca. Their only hope of powerful support was now Charles of Valois, pretender to the throne of Byzantium, whose emissary, Admiral Thibaut de Cepoy, was before them. With very little argument the decision was taken, homage sworn to the 'Emperor' Charles and Thibaut accepted as commander-in-chief.

The third resolution was a vote of thanks to Muntaner, who had not been compensated for his time, effort or expense and who had worked only for the common weal; it ended by recommending him to 'our Lord Emperor Charles'. The minutes of the meeting, as they may be called, are dated at Cassandria on 11 August 1307. A transcript is preserved with the Catania copy of Muntaner's manuscript in the University Library of that city.

Once Thibaut had been accepted as head of the Company there was nothing to detain the Venetian galleys, which consequently left for Negroponte, taking Muntaner with them. He presented Thibaut's request that his stolen goods should be returned, and the order was given. But like so many of Thibaut's orders it was wind and no more, befitting a captain whose master was 'a king of the hat and the wind'. The dutiful Muntaner now asked, and received, permission to go to Thebes to visit the imprisoned Prince Ferdinand. He rode in a party of five and presented himself to the Duke of Athens, who normally resided in the castle of Cadmeia. He found him ill, suffering in fact from the disease which was to kill him a year later; but well or ill, he had not lost the courtesy for which he was famed. He declared himself desolated at Muntaner's bad luck and asked how he might best serve him. The Catalan replied that the greatest pleasure the duke could give him would be in treating the captive prince with all honour. He further asked permission to visit him and the duke replied that he could not only see him but stay with him and that, in Muntaner's honour, as long as the visit lasted, anyone he wished could come and go and could dine with the prince and that if he wished to go out riding he could do so.

'And straightway they opened the gates of the Castle of St Omer, where the Prince was, and I went to see him. And I had such sorrow when I saw him in the power of others that I thought my heart would break.'[13] His sympathy, in fact, was so strong that the captive did all the comforting while Muntaner could only weep. During the two days they were together the prince wrote a letter of recommendation to his cousin Frederick, King of Sicily, and assured himself that Muntaner had a verbal message by heart. In this way Frederick was to learn of the failure of Ferdinand's mission and the reason why. Sick at heart, Muntaner finally took leave of the prince and then of the Duke of Athens. The latter courteously made him accept valuable jewels, all the more welcome as Muntaner had left all his money with the prisoner and had divided his spare raiment among the attendants; the cook came in for special bounty, in return for which he swore on the gospels that he would sooner let himself be beheaded than allow any noxious thing to be put in the prince's food, while Muntaner on his part swore to reward him well if he remained faithful to his trust.

I have dwelt on this episode, as it is one of the few in the lamentable history of the Catalan Company that does not end in treachery and bloodshed. Prince Ferdinand was sent to Robert of Naples after a short time and was kept there in nominal captivity only, which was to be expected as the queen was Ferdinand's sister. It seems likely that he acquainted King Robert with Rocafort's part in his, Ferdinand's, abortive visit to the Company; as we shall see in chapter 9 Robert was in any case no friend of Rocafort. After a year's pleasant stay, hunting with the king and eating at the royal table, Ferdinand was sent back to Mallorca, but the impetuous prince was not thus to be deprived of adventure. He was to meet his death on Greek soil, during his next expedition.

Muntaner did not return to the Company but served his king diligently in other fields. He eventually retired loaded with honours, but not before he had the opportunity of serving his royal and hot-headed friend once more.[14] Of the man himself much has been written. To many, the account of his leave-taking from the Company and his subsequent return, describing with modest pride how officers and men, Almugavars and Turks, competed in doing him honour, will be sufficient evidence of his character. The siege of Gallipoli witnesses his courage, the visit to Ferdinand at Thebes his warm-heartedness. Of his work, the fairest tribute is paid by Buchon, his French translator. Writing of the Catalan expedition to the East, he says:

> All this part of Muntaner's chronicle is written with as much accuracy as talent. Facts, places, men are portrayed to the life in their true aspect. I have carefully compared his account with those of the Greek authors of the day and I have always found in Muntaner the superiority, not only of a more judicious spirit and a firmer character, but of a more impartial judgment of his enemies and a more thorough and resolute respect for the truth . . .

How much Muntaner's chronicle owes to Villehardouin, his predecessor by a century, we shall never know. But there is no doubt that, as men and as writers, they were less than kin but more than kind. Of Villehardouin, the chronicler of the fourth Crusade, Sir Frank Marzials writes:[15]

> A man, evidently like Scott's William of Deloraine, 'good at need'—a man trusted of all and trustworthy—honoured by the Doge, honoured by the Emperor Baldwin, honoured and beloved by the Marquis of Montferrat. Nor should it be imagined, because this is the impression left by a study of the

chronicle, that Villehardouin's method of telling the story of the Crusade has in it anything of personal boastfulness or vainglory. When he speaks of himself, in the course of the narrative, he does so quite simply, and just as he speaks of others. There is no attempt to magnify his own deeds or influence. If he has taken part in any adventure or deliberation, he mentions the fact without false modesty, but does not dwell upon it unduly. And, indeed, as I read the man's character, a certain honourable straightforwardness seems to me one of its most important traits.

I can think of no more fitting portrayal of Muntaner than the above and could certainly not present it with equal elegance.

Chapter 9

The third lost leader
1308–10

Thibaut had already reached Negroponte when Prince Ferdinand arrived at Gallipoli, and he had instituted secret negotiations with Rocafort, who was busy at the siege of Nona.[1] With this fact in mind Rocafort's behaviour is more easily understood for, after Entenza's death, there was really no reason why he should reject Ferdinand as a figurehead. He was confident enough that he would remain the real commander when homage had been paid to Thibaut; he had no reason to doubt, earlier on, that his position would be equally strong under Ferdinand. But he may have already obtained concessions from Thibaut for his personal advantage and may even have concluded a secret pact. If this were so he could certainly not tolerate the presence of the Mallorcan prince.

Speculation is necessary in this and in much that follows, for the chroniclers of the years 1307 to 1310 are few and unreliable. Muntaner was absent and obtained the facts, so far as they were known, from one Arnal de Caza in 1316.[2] Gregoras was never present and in fact wrote about fifty years later. Theodulos Magister and the Serbian Archbishop Daniel II, who witnessed a few of the episodes, give short accounts with vague references.

On the map of the Northern Aegean a curiously shaped promontory stands out. It is mountainous and rugged and terminates in three narrow tongues of land, the whole being known as Chalkidike. The tongue on the east is the promontory of Athos, where flourishing monastic communities were already established. The central one, Longos, need not concern us. Cassandria is situated on the western arm, very near the ancient and at that time forgotten town of Potidaea. Geographically, Cassandria made an ideal base, its situation at the neck of a tongue of land being reminiscent of Gallipoli and Cyzicus. Like Gallipoli too it dominated large tracts of fertile land and was so situated as to be a threat to an important city, not Constantinople this time, but Salonika or Thessalonika.

To reach Cassandria Christopolis had to be by-passed, because the Byzantines had built a wall from the sea to Mt Rhodope, in an attempt to contain the Company's raiding parties;[3] the army, with its women, children and sick, therefore took the arduous path over the slopes of Rhodope. The straggling throng, negotiating narrow mountain passes and picking its way over precipitous escarpments, must have made a tempting prize for the Greek forces; we shall never know why they were not ambushed.

By this time the fighting men of all nations numbered some 8,000 and Rocafort, as sole Catalan leader, surviving to inherit the commands of Roger de Flor, Aonés, Corberán, Entenza and Jiménez, was a proud man indeed. As so often in history, rapid access to power from humble origins induced that blend of arrogance and recklessness that the Greeks called 'hubris'. Rocafort's pride irritated his captains and even his own supporters began to lose the affection which the deeds of this great leader had inspired. He became ever more autocratic as time went on and after Muntaner's second departure it became plain that Thibaut had no authority, except through Rocafort, and that the distant Charles of Valois was once again 'king of the hat and the wind'. Thibaut was in fact a prisoner and Rocafort 'treated him like a dog' and 'regarded him less than a sergeant', to borrow contemporary phrases.

The reason is not far to seek: Rocafort, having served under Peter the Great as well as his sons James II and Frederick III, resented the colourless representative of an inglorious pretender. At the same time Rocafort, who is presumed to have married Roger de Flor's daughter,[4] prided himself on his connection with that great man, beside whom all other leaders were insignificant. I have called Thibaut colourless; perhaps his very mediocrity was his strongest weapon. We must bear this in mind while we watch the hidden struggle for power.

With pride went ambition. A pocket Napoleon, Rocafort entertained the project of making himself King of Thessalonika and had already ordered a seal bearing the effigy of a crowned horseman, presumably St Demetrios, patron of the city. He also arranged to have a golden crown made and, true to type, began negotiations for a marriage above his social stratum. The bride he had in mind[5] was Jeanette de Brienne, half sister of Guy II de la Roche, Duke of Athens. It is an indication of the importance which the Catalan Company had obtained that his offer was taken seriously; Guy sent two of his minstrels to Cassandria as envoys and seems to have toyed with the idea of employing the Company to further claims of his own in the Morea.

Jeannette's value as a bargaining piece was considerable and Guy had already been approached with a proposal from another quarter. The senior empress of Byzantium was Irene,[6] second wife of Andronicus II (see p. 18). She resented the fact that Michael IX and the other descendants of Andronicus' first marriage had precedence over her own children and, enraged at being unable to alter imperial rules of succession, had left her husband in Constantinople and was living in Salonika. Her son Theodore was now titular Marquis of Montferrat; the title had descended to him from Boniface, second in precedence only to the Latin emperors of Constantinople,* and his mother felt that he should regain the family lands in Thessaly. But Thessaly belonged to another Byzantine prince, young John II Angelos, ward of Guy de la Roche. Irene's idea, that she and the duke should cement an alliance with the marriage of Theodore and Jeannette and then make a concerted attack on young John, was repugnant to Guy, whose political morality was quite exceptional.

Ambitions and intrigues did not interfere with the normal routine of the Catalan Company. The Vengeance was still being inflicted on the unprotected countryside but lack of siege engines continued to render vain their attempts on fortified places. The city of Salonika, second greatest of the Empire, was now the residence of both empresses, Irene wife of Andronicus and Maria, wife of his son Michael IX.[7] It was defended by the Greek general Chandrinos, who was later to break the uninterrupted succession of Catalan victories in the open field.

Thwarted in his attempt to capture Salonika—perhaps due to his savage threats and insistence on unconditional surrender—Rocafort now changed his objective. He led his men against Mt Athos on the eastern promontory of Chalkidike; they crossed the narrow neck,

* See Prologue.

with its traces of Xerxes' ship canal; they saw the monasteries twinkling on the dark, sheer slopes and they thought of the wealth that they contained. It was in the autumn of 1307 that they climbed to the first attack on the richest storehouse of Byzantine wealth. A few smaller communities were overrun, but the only effect of this was that in future the monks would site their dwellings and churches in more defensible places. The main attack was against the Monastery of Chilandarios on the north coast, but here the walls were so high and the monks so resolute that every attempt at carrying the buildings by assault failed. The abbott, or *higoumenos* (who was to be the future Archbishop Daniel II), and several of his priors sent a deputation to Catalonia; on 1 July James II of Aragón was able to give an assurance that he had ordered the Company to cease molesting them.[8] But why should the Company obey the commands of a king who disowned them? Sporadic raids lasted for nearly two years more. James had incidentally written to Rocafort on 10 May, encouraging vigorous support of Charles of Valois and Thibaut. There was no monotony about the policies of the rulers of those days.

Rocafort was now becoming ever more despotic. The feeling that he was the undisputed chief of the dreaded Almugavars more than offset the failure of the attack on Mt Athos and the continued resistance of Salonika. This was actually more than passive resistance. The emperors of Byzantium, fearing for their wives—(or possibly the ransom they might have to pay for them)—had sent the redoubtable General Chandrinos. Fresh from triumphs in Asia, this Greek soldier took the measure of the Catalan Company and inflicted on them one defeat after another, recovering an enormous amount of booty. It seems as though even the nominal leadership of Thibaut de Cepoy had a weakening influence on the Almugavars; Rocafort would in any case blame the Frenchman rather than his own defective strategy.

The summation of Rocafort's increasing tyranny and his reverses in the field made many enemies among the Almugavars. Essentially democratic in the management of their own affairs, they resented a ruler more capricious than any monarch. Complaints became ever more frequent as Rocafort appropriated the goods of every man dying on active service, while wives, mistresses and daughters were no longer safe from his lust. It was the pattern that the declining Roman empire saw so frequently, that of the self-made man who could rule others but not himself.

Thibaut, who had long ago resolved to bring down the tyrant, felt the growing resentment round him. He sounded out other officers and, convinced of the support of fourteen of them, called for a meeting of the Council. Well rehearsed, they waited until Rocafort and his brother swaggered in. Then, with the first motion of the agenda, they began to complain of his behaviour. As one after another rose to criticize him, Rocafort's anger mounted. Accustomed to having his orders obeyed without question and new to criticism from those he had come to regard as his servants, he treated the accusations with his habitual insolence.

The fourteen captains, at a prearranged signal, surged forward, crowding round Bernard de Rocafort and his brother Gisbert. As they did so their complaints became louder and their attitude more menacing. Suddenly the tumult was stilled and the onlookers saw the Rocafort brothers bound and being hustled away to the galleys. These were Thibaut's own, and there is every likelihood that he had planned the *coup* to coincide with their return from Venice under his brother's command.

There was rejoicing at the downfall of a tyrant and, as we have followed the fortunes of the Catalan Company for six years, we are not surprised to read that his house was promptly and thoroughly sacked. Its contents, incidentally, were so rich that the share-out yielded thirteen gold *bezants* to each man. The prisoners were placed in Thibaut's galleys and sent to Italy; we cannot be certain of their number, but the wording of the accounts suggests that others beside the Rocaforts were included. Their uncle Dalmau de San Martín had died some months before.

Muntaner, who of course was no longer an eyewitness and therefore less reliable, states that Thibaut himself accompanied the prisoners, and other authors accepted the statement until last century; then Rubió i Lluch made a careful study of the Byzantine historians, puzzled no doubt by the fact that Thibaut should leave the interests of Charles of Valois so summarily. It is now known that he stayed on with the Company for more than a year.

By Thibaut's orders the prisoners were delivered to King Robert of Naples, grandson of Charles of Anjou, 'good King Robert' as they called him. A typical Angevin, he neither forgot nor forgave. He wanted them, says the chronicler, 'more than anyone in the world, for the castles of Calabria, which they had not wanted to return, as did the others' (Chapter 3). Now he was able to indulge the family partiality for mean revenge, of which Roger de Flor's childhood gave a good example. The Rocafort brothers were sent to the Castle of Aversa, near Naples, walled up under an arch in the cellar and left there to die of hunger and thirst in their eternal night.

So perished miserably yet another commander-in-chief of the Catalan Company, victim of his own greed and arrogance. His ambition for a crown in Thessalonika ended precisely as did Roger de Flor's for the fief of Anatolia and more besides. It was an age when boldness and brains could advance a man just so far; the Establishment saw to it that he was liquidated when he raised his eyes to a throne. His heroism, determination, leadership and brilliancy are still alive while the memory of his greed and arrogance grows dim. He represents an epoch in the legendary history of Catalonia, land of heroes. Says Nicolau d'Olwer: 'Without him a whole chapter of our life would lack a representative hero. As epitaph for the buried seneschal, Thibaut is to enter this item in his account book, "To Jacques de Cornoy, who conveyed to Apulia Rocafort and other traitors, and from there went to France, sixty florins".'

The situation of the Company in Cassandria was now becoming desperate. Their ravages had as usual denuded the countryside within striking distance and longer forays were too dangerous to risk against Chandrinos; and not Chandrinos only, but a new offensive spirit in the Greeks. St Demetrios, it was said, rode at the head of their troops and assured them victory. Stimulated by hunger the Catalans could only move on; repeating their departure from Gallipoli, therefore, they decided to move west into Thessaly. We can imagine Thibaut's feelings as his turbulent force moved further away from the capital they were being paid to attack. But they could not return to Thrace, for the Greeks had blocked the road through Christopolis; they therefore raised the siege of Salonika and made a dash for Thessaly in the spring of 1309, completing thirty hours' march in three days, but not without suffering two defeats. But they passed the barrier of Mt Olympus and made their camp in the Vale of Tempe. It was a march into the unknown, characterized by Nikephoros Gregoras, for what his opinion is worth, as an act of folly rather than boldness. By luck or design, however, they found themselves in the delightful gorge that separates Ossa from Olympus. In the coolness under the planes and willows that line the banks of the River Peneios, the host took its leisure through the summer, horses and mules cropping the lush meadow grass, some of the women and prisoners no doubt delighting in the scent of laurel and jasmine and the cool, calm waters of the river. But the spectacular contrast between the smiling valley and the bare, towering mountains was hardly likely to promote in the breasts of the Catalans the religious awe which made the valley sacred in the eyes of the ancient Greeks, to Apollo and to his son Aristaeos, guardian of fruit trees and cattle.

Under Thibaut the men raided inland, but the days of easy conquest and unopposed pillage were over; so too was the dash and resolution of the old Almugavars. Now they were matched against the savage mountaineers of central Thessaly, Wallachians and Slavs as well as Greeks, and many a raid was bloodily repulsed. Their chief opponent was still the redoubtable Chandrinos, whose strategy consisted in denying the Catalans access to the interior.

Luckily, however, the death of Guy de la Roche in October of 1303 left his protégé, the sebastokrator or Grand Duke of Neopatras,[9] John II Angelos, without a protector. Attempting to find a substitute for the former Frankish support he had arranged to marry another Irene; this one was probably the grand-daughter of Andronicus II (see p.18). In spite of matrimony, however, John was still exposed to the menace of his neighbours, grouped like vultures round a dying ox.

It is difficult to make a coherent story out of the young sebastokrator's catalogue of stupidities. It seems that John's matrimonial alliance with Byzantium provoked Walter of Brienne, the new Duke of Athens, who felt that John should continue to be his ward; as such he would be nominal ruler of the most fertile province of Greece and a valuable buffer against invaders. At the same time the Byzantine Empire, largely because of the damage done by the Catalan Company, was going through one of its periodic phases of apparently falling to pieces. Chandrinos was now recalled in disgrace; we do not know why, but we can remember that this was a frequent consequence of success among Byzantine generals, probably as an example of imperial fright. The young sebastokrator thought he would be in the fashion, set by other dependents, if he defied Andronicus, his new protector. Among other rapacious neighbours John could count the Empress Irene at Salonika, who had not given up the idea of establishing her son in Thessaly. You may be sure that there were more. Of all the vultures the Catalans were the nearest; but they were also open to the persuasion of pay. Thibaut therefore arranged for the Company to be employed by the weakling sebastokrator and they were thus able to pass the winter of 1309 in mythological surroundings and financial security.

In the spring of 1310 the Company resumed its ravaging expeditions, unable as usual to distinguish friend from foe when anything of value could be picked up. Thibaut had become disillusioned regarding the loyalty of the Catalans to their paymaster and saw clearly that their depredations would not make their nominal employer, Charles of Valois, more popular in Greece. Here we are faced with a difficulty. Catherine de Courtenay, whose claim to the throne of Byzantium was being pressed by her husband, Charles of Valois, had died in the spring of 1308. Her claim had descended to the eldest of her three daughters, Catherine of Valois; it was the latter's husband, Prince Philip of Taranto, who was now officially entitled to claim Byzantium on his wife's behalf and, as he was the younger brother of 'good' King Robert, the House of Anjou had for some months replaced the House of Valois as claimants. Perhaps Charles wanted to pursue his other claim, through his first wife; nothing would be too fanciful for the 'king of the hat and the wind'.

It is strange that the Company remained ignorant of this important change; perhaps politics were too complicated for them. To us it is hardly surprising that Thibaut would now leave the Company, nor that he would make his departure as unobtrusive as possible. He had many reasons for leaving. Nothing had been done to implement the proposed conquest of Constantinople; his authority was weak; and finally there had been the usual dispute about pay, for the Company, so he said, had demanded money for services not rendered. It is true that he had now arranged to put the Company at the disposal of Walter of Brienne, with the object of making conquests in Thessaly for the duchy of Athens, but he must surely have preferred the life of a high official in France to that of a condottiere in Greece. It was early in 1310 that he made off, for we find a mention of his presence in Senlis on 29 April of that year.

So it was that the troops awoke one morning to find their commander gone. After the first shock of surprise the men gave way to anger. Intrigues and subtleties were little to the taste of these rude soldiers, whose way of settling an argument was face to face, sword or lance in hand. A stealthy absconding, such as this, was beyond

I

their experience. Thrice coward, they called him, and their indignation mounted as they remembered that it was through this
foreigner that they had lost their Rocafort, the fearless Rocafort. So
quickly does kindly time obliterate distasteful memories. Could they
but lay their hands on Thibaut they would soon avenge their idol.
Balked of this revenge they turned in rage on the fourteen captains
who had handed Rocafort over to Thibaut, and dispatched them
with lance thrusts in an instant. Then they paused to mourn the
leader whose arrogance they had so resented last year and they wept
as they remembered the victories they had won, and forgot the
defeats they had suffered, during the years he had commanded
them. They could not but compare their diminished fortunes in
Thessaly with the easy prizes of yore.

Without a competent head the Company was nothing, and now
there was no one to take the place of Rocafort, or even Thibaut.
They therefore elected a committee of four, two knights, an *adalid*
and an *almocadén*; its decisions were subject to the approval of the
Council of Twelve that survived from Gallipoli days, and under this
primitive form of democracy the Company went on to a future more
fantastic than any of them could conceive.

It was the spring of 1310, wild flowers flaunted their colours over
every mountain slope and the verdant folds of Thessaly's rich plains
proclaimed that the foraging would be good. But the Company
would be elsewhere. Exactly how and when it parted from its employer, the sebastokrator, is not recorded; indeed some say that they
were never in his employ and that the money he gave them was a
bribe, accompanied by trusty guides, to get them over the mountains and out of his territory. If this is true, the Catalan Company
should go down in history as one of the earliest exponents of the
protection racket. Of their methods we gain an unexpected glimpse
in the story of St Athanasios the Meteorite. His title suggests an
astronaut, but he was very much down to earth, instituting the strict,
indeed harsh rule of the Meteoron; today we see a picturesque
huddle of monasteries crowning Thessalian hill tops in a bizarre
jumble of rocky columns, pinnacles and crags. Athanasios was captured by the Company when he was five years old and taken along
with them. The child may thus have accompanied his captors from
the neighbourhood of Mt Othrys, where he had been seized,
through all the fertile parts of Thessaly.[10] It is a pity that he never
wrote an account of his experiences, though he became educated

after leaving his captors, for none of this episode of its wanderings has been described by an eyewitness.[11]

The Catalan depredations in Thessaly had been so ruinous during the previous year that the inhabitants decided to ask the help of the Byzantine emperors. Now the raiders had lost Rocafort and the Greeks still had Chalandrinos. The Galaxidi Chronicle,[12] which incidentally calls him Andreas or Andrikos, summarizes events as follows:

After a long time there came letters and *bullae* [decrees] from the emperor, stating that many fearful corsairs, whom they name Taragonatas,[13] had come to seize the imperial lands by force of arms. The emperor, desirous of striking terror into those pirates, sent letters and decrees to the lands of Rumelia and Morea, warning them all to arm, old and young, and hurry against the corsairs. He promised them moreover that those countries that obeyed the imperial mandate and threw their forces against the Taragonatas, would pay no tribute and would in future be self-governing, and would be favoured with other gifts and credits. All obeyed the imperial order and there were armed up to three thousand fighters from Epaktos,[14] Galaxidion, Lidorikion and other towns, who came against the corsairs; but on gathering at the camp of Zituni [Lamia] their leaders fell out. They abused each other shamefully, wanted to go their own ways and nearly came to blows. But the men of Galaxidion placed themselves under the lord Andreas, one of the emperor's best generals, who fought two magnificent battles, in which he killed many corsairs, and they soon returned to Galaxidion with many gifts from the lord Andronicus. But thereafter the corsairs, due to the discord and divisions between the Greeks, took possession of many cities without opposition, among them Salona.

Salona (Amphissa) possessed one of the strongest castles of the time and was to be the seat of the last relic of Spanish power on the Grecian mainland. How the Catalans got down to this part of Greece can best be explained by assuming that the Thessalians had bribed them to cross the Phourkas Pass over Mt Othrys, to Lamia. This may have been the occasion of their kidnapping Athanasios the future Meteorite. The places mentioned in the Galaxidi Chronicle are all near or on the north coast of the Gulf of Corinth, a considerable distance from Thessaly.

Greek successes were so few, and those of the Catalans so many, that the victories of Chandrinos aroused disproportionate enthusiasm among his compatriots. One of the few writers who were eye-witnesses of the events of 1310—perhaps the only one—was Theodulos Magister, or the Rhetorician, whose letters imitate the style, without achieving the accuracy of Thucydides. Two surviving fragments from his pen refer to the Catalan Company and one of them mentions that their defeats by Chandrinos in Thessaly were even in his day 'sung by the Thessalians and nearly all men'.[15] All this convinces us, if indeed we need convincing, that the terror inspired by the Catalans was one of their most powerful weapons. The German phrase *'das psychologische Moment'* was coined to mean just that, the factor which affects the enemy's morale, itself (according to Napoleon) the important three-quarters of warfare.[16]

Chapter 10

The final triumph
1310-11

The fourth Crusade was but the memory of a century ago and Frankish Greece, having passed the time in senseless quarrels was now divided roughly as follows: *The Morea*, or Peloponnese, was largely the property of the Angevins, who had won the tenure of the Princes of Achaia; *Athens and Thebes* were the principal cities of the rich and influential Duchy of Athens; the Venetians held most of *Negroponte (Euboea)* and the Greeks retained the rest. *Thrace and Macedonia* belonged to Byzantium and *Epiros* survived as an independent Greek despotate.

During their occupation the Franks, especially the French and Burgundians, had transplanted the seed of western chivalry into fertile soil. Achaia became the transmitter and later the leader of courtly tradition, so that young aristocrats from western Europe went there to complete their education as gentle knights at a court where a French not inferior to that of Paris was spoken. Of all the schools of chivalry in the east, that at Lacedaemonia, the ancient Sparta, was pre-eminent and France sent her pupils to learn at a court 'more brilliant than that of a great king', as it was commonly termed. To French ears the soft Greek language was at first quite unintelligible and, ignorant of the classical fame which place names commemorated, they altered them to suit their own taste. Thus Lacedaemonia became *La Crémonie*, Monemvasia *Malevasie*, Kalavryta *La Grite* and Larissa *L'Arse*. Frankish Greece, in fact, became a repository of the French spirit, an example of French brilliance in battle and the pride of the mother country.

During the Frankish conquest of Greece that followed the fourth Crusade, Boniface de Montferrat conferred the territories of Boeotia and Attica, with their capitals Thebes and Athens, on his Burgundian comrade Othon de la Roche (see Prologue). The title 'Duke of Athens' has an interesting history,[1] evolving from Othon as self-styled *dominus*, through Μέγας κύριος to 'Grand Duke', as authorized by Louis IX. Thereafter it is understandable that the title should be made retrospective; Dante bestowed it on Theseus, Muntaner on Menelaos,[2] and Boccaccio, Chaucer and Shakespeare again on Theseus. At the time of the Catalan invasion the bearer of the title was counted among the noblest of rulers below the rank of prince.

The Court of Athens, which actually spent its time at Thebes, was not outdone in splendour by that of La Crémonie. The smiths knew how to gild and the looms of Thebes wove gorgeously coloured silks and satins, to which the art of their Greek and Jewish craftsmen added golden threads. It is not surprising that Roger II of Sicily had sent his admiral, George of Antioch, to kidnap a number of weavers and bring them to Palermo. The brilliant court witnessed one episode which concerns our story; it took place at the coming of age of Guy II de la Roche—the last de la Roche—on Midsummer's Day, 1294. Muntaner tells the story.[3] After mass in the Cathedral of Thebes, the young duke stood by the altar on which his arms rested and looked about him for someone of sufficient honour and nobility to give him the accolade of knighthood. His glance passed over the great lords of Salona and St Omer and rested on Bonifacio dalle Carceri da Verona, youngest son of a famous family. He had sold his only castle in order to come to Greece; once there he had lived for seven years in princely style without visible means of support. But Guy knew him for a faithful friend.

'Sir Bonifacio,' said he, 'stay here next the Archbishop, for I will that you dub me knight.'

'Ah, Lord!' replied Bonifacio. 'What do you say? Would you mock me?'

'Indeed no, but thus I wish it to be.'

And so it was. Then the duke announced that though it was customary for a knight to make a present to the squire he had dubbed, in this instance the reverse would be done. He then loaded Bonifacio with gifts, not the least of them a wealthy wife, his

cousin Agnes de Cicon. The anecdote has relevance, in that Bonifacio was Muntaner's host when Prince Ferdinand and he had been
taken by the Venetians; we may assume that the chronicler heard
the story from the other's lips and we note, in the light of future
events, that the Italian was well disposed to the Catalans, perhaps
as a result of entertaining a great Catalan gentleman.

I have mentioned the death of Guy II de la Roche in November
1308. He bequeathed the duchy to Walter de Brienne, Count of
Lecce, who was both his cousin and step-brother. The Briennes
were a family whose adventurous spirit was remarkable, even for
that age, as was their reckless bravery. His great-grandfather
Walter was a pretender to the throne of Sicily and consequently died
in prison. His grandfather, another Walter, was captured by the
Saracens, hung by the arms before his own castle of Jaffa and died
steadfastly refusing to order the garrison to surrender. His father,
Hugh de Brienne, was one of the 300 French 'knights of death' who
refused quarter at the battle of Gagliano in Sicily and were killed to
a man. So it was with Walter too; before recounting the supreme
test of the Catalan Grand Company we at least have the measure of
its opponent.

I discussed the peculiar position of the sebastokrator, John
Angelos, Duke of Neopatras, in the last chapter. Once the Catalans
had been got rid of he found himself exposed to the threat of an even
more powerful Duke of Athens, and to the ambitions of Byzantium
and the Greek despotate of Epiros, ruled by the haughty and
acquisitive Lady Anna. An ephemeral truce was negotiated and the
three ill-assorted Greek parties, Byzantium, Epiros and Neopatras,
joined to resist the aspirations of the new Duke of Athens. It was
not the first time that a Duke of Athens had thought of employing
the Catalan Company (readers will remember the two minstrels of
Guy de la Roche who came to discuss terms with Rocafort) and
Walter of Brienne was no stranger to the Almugavars. For years he
had been a prisoner in the Castle of Augusta, in Sicily, and had even
learned to speak Catalan, while a child hostage for his father. A
second link had been forged during the three years that Jiménez
d'Arenós and his men were in the service of the late duke. Now
Walter made use of the services of a knight on his staff, Roger
Deslaur of Roussillon, as an envoy, a service which was to stand
him in good stead. Catalan was his native language and we may infer
that he was soon on good terms with the Catalans.

The Company, weary with the hardships of its latest journey and dispirited by its repulses at the hands of Chandrinos, was well disposed to Walter's emissary. There is some evidence that he was only one of several envoys from interested states, bidding for the services of the mercenaries; this is possibly why the terms they were offered, and eventually accepted, were so generous. According to some, they insisted on waiting in Thessaly until their contract had been signed and sworn (they were still simple soldiers, with all the simple man's faith in oaths and documents, for all that they had a council and a committee of management); others say that the negotiations took place after crossing Phourkas Pass and making camp near Zituni. On one fact all chroniclers were agreed: that the Company was engaged and the terms agreed on freely by both parties.

Their pay had not altered in eight years: four ounces of gold per month for each armed horseman, two for the light horse and one for the infantry. The contract stipulated employment for six months, of which the first two were paid in advance. Campaigning began, according to their agreement, with the spring of 1310 and once more achieved the brilliancy of the Company's earlier exploits. At this time they numbered between 6,000 and 7,000 and in 1310 they were accompanied by the still more numerous Athenian army, possibly provided with siege engines, of which the Company had none. On 6 June we hear of them besieging Zituni; turning back, they recrossed the Phourkas Pass, took Domokos and debouched on to the plain of Thessaly. Once more this was subjected to their depredations, in spite of all the efforts of the uneasy alliance of the three Greek states.

In the stipulated six months their assignment had been completed; the enemy sued for peace and Walter found himself the owner of thirty castles surrendered to the arms and reputation of the Catalans. He dictated his own peace terms, which his opponents were glad to accept. The presence of the Company in Thessaly had two direct consequences: the exports of Thessaly declined sharply; and Clement V ordered the expropriated (then as now a better word than 'stolen') revenues of the suppressed Order of Templars to be lent to the Church's 'faithful champion against the schismatic Greeks'. For one of their few, brief interludes, the Catalans found themselves on the side of the angels.

But now they received a shock. They had thought to finish their odyssey at last and to settle in the fertile plains of Boeotia as farmer-frontier guards. Not only did Walter refuse to allow them to stay on in his duchy; he would not even let them pass through to the Morea, where they might carve themselves a homeland from the territory of the hated Angevins. The reason was perhaps that the Briennes, in their fief of Lecce, were themselves vassals of the Angevin Robert of Naples. And now Walter felt himself so secure, with his own army mobilized and with every road and mountain pass dominated by one of his own castles, that he made the fatal mistake of trying to swindle the Catalan Company. As usual the question of booty was the excuse for withholding their wages, for they had received nothing since the two months' advance of salary. Did their booty belong to them or their employer? To the mercenary soldier there was only one answer.

The pattern should by now have become familiar to the Catalans. When their employers were in desperate straits no inducement was too expensive, if it had a chance of obtaining their services. Once the danger was past their extravagant rates of pay were seen in the cold light of reality and every expedient adopted to default. Frederick of Sicily, it is true, was a man of honour and dealing with his own compatriots, but even he could not disguise his satisfaction at getting rid of the Catalan Company with the utmost dispatch when it was no longer needed. Andronicus had tried to withhold their pay, then sent depreciated money and finally connived at the treacherous murder of Roger de Flor and his companions.

Walter de Brienne could not imagine that what had happened to Greeks during the Catalan Vengeance could happen to him and his conquering Franks. His commitments were now over 12,000 gold ounces per month in pay alone, at a rough guess, the equivalent of £170,000. Like Andronicus, he tried to get out of his obligations in two ways: first, as we have seen, by repudiating his debt for back pay by trying to set it off against the Company's loot; and secondly by terminating their service. This he was perfectly entitled to do, and indeed so was Andronicus, for the one had engaged them for six months and the other for nine. Had Walter therefore settled the arrears of pay there could have been no objection to dismissing them at the end of six months.

What he actually did was to engage the pick of the Company, 22 horse and 300 foot, pay them what he owed them and establish them as landed gentry. He ordered the rest to get out of his territory, giving them but a short time to do so, and threatening to treat them as rebels and enemies if they refused. The phrase that the Spanish chroniclers put in his mouth is equivalent to telling them to go to the devil.[4] Still acting with moderation, the Company's spokesmen declared that they were ready to go as soon as they received their arrears of pay, with which they proposed to purchase vessels and return to their own country. The duke flatly refused and added that he had nothing for them but the gibbet. With such arrogance and such insults did he address them that even the Greek historian Gregoras was amazed;[5] he concluded that Walter intended to annihilate the Company as a prelude to a ravaging campaign through imperial territory and up to the gates of Constantinople. Once more the spokesmen of the Company, with unwonted forbearance, offered an alternative: if the duke would allow them to remain— for they really had nowhere else to go[6]—they would do homage for, and occupy the castles they had won in southern Thessaly. Again they were contemptuously ordered to leave the duchy of Athens and threatened with the might of the Frankish chivalry, 'the finest cavalry in the world' as Nicolau d'Olwer described them.[7]

It has been largely overlooked that the Duke of Athens had more than one strong inducement to get the Spaniards out of his territory. In that same year of 1310 Andronicus and the Venetians had signed a commercial treaty in which appeared the following clause: 'Under pain of severe penalty, it is forbidden to any Venetian subject to trade with the Catalan Company, while it forcibly occupies any part of the Empire.'[8] By continuing to employ them, therefore, Walter of Brienne was threatened with the hostility and economic sanctions of the powerful republic which, as overlord of Negroponte, was a close and dangerous neighbour.

Sullenly the mercenaries went back to winter in Thessaly. They reinforced their numbers by enlisting some of their prisoners (was Athanasios the Meteorite among them?) as archers and passed the time in raiding the surrounding districts, on which they were now forced to live. Walter, on his part, did everything to ensure that the coming year would see him rid of the troublesome upstarts, among whom there was now not a single officer of gentle birth. Like Porsena of Clusium, 'he named a trysting day, and made his messengers ride forth, east and west and south and north, to summon his array.' And not only his own array, but those of the cream of the Frankish barons.

A Debrett of Greece would have been fairly represented by the powerful contingents that came to swell the army of the Duke of Athens. There was Albert Pallavicini, whose ancestor had marched with Boniface de Montferrat, and whose castle of Boudonitza dominated the historic defile of Thermopylae. Thomas III de Stromoncourt, Count of Salona, left his ancient castle at Amphissa to bring his troops to the rallying point. Reginald de la Roche came from the Morea, and his father, Anthony the Fleming, Lord of Carditza. From Negroponte came our friend Bonifacio da Verona, now a wealthy and influential baron; Jean de Maisy, who had custody of Prince Ferdinand while Muntaner lodged with Bonifacio; and George Ghisi, who numbered the islands of Tenos and Mykonos among his possessions. The Angevins sent their noble vassals from the Morea and even from the kingdom of Naples, while the men of the Cyclades sailed to Attica under the banner of their lord, the Duke of Naxos. Never since the historic tournament of Corinth in 1305 had Greece seen such an array of gallant men, eager to close with the Almugavars and Turks, from whom, in spite of their low estate, much honour could be gained.

In the early spring the Catalan Company left its winter quarters in Thessaly and returned to the Boetian plain, which they had selected as the setting for what might well be their last battle. They travelled with women and children and with all their baggage, and this time selected the coast road through Thermopylae, passing below the frowning walls of the Pallavicini stronghold of Boudonitza. It would of course have been easy to contain them here, or at Kallidromos, or Purnaraki Pass, but this was not the Frankish strategy, if the word may be fairly used. It was Walter of Brienne's aim to rid the world once and for all of the pernicious Catalans. Let them walk into the trap. Whether his plan was sound or not, it is difficult to say; certainly the subsequent tactics were woefully deficient.

The Company turned inland and skirted the northern shore of Lake Copais, today drained and cultivated, where cotton and wheat grow between the lush meadows of Greece's richest plain. In the fourteenth century it was a broad sheet of water, fed at its western end by the river Kephissos. This the Catalan Company crossed, stationing themselves so that the lake protected one flank. On their left were the ruins of ancient Orchomenos, where Iasos had lorded it in the days before the Trojan war; and to the right lay Chaeronea, site of Greece's fall before the onslaught of Philip of Macedon and

Alexander the Great. Many other battles had been decided hereabouts, but surely none so strange as that which was to follow.

Western tactics in those days were simple and consisted in exploiting the superiority of heavily armed horsemen over infantry or light cavalry. The invention of the stirrup, the introduction of plate armour and the breeding of sturdier mounts, ancestors of the Clydesdales, Shire horses and Percherons of today, all had the object of making the *cavalier*, or horseman, irresistible. He might well be, when faced with lightly armed infantry in open country, but he became helpless when his opponents used new weapons—the Anglo-Welsh longbow comes to mind—or their brains. It thus happened that at the peak of the age of chivalry the armoured knight was obsolescent; in less than a thousand years he had recapitulated the million years of the great Saurians. Like them, his armour grew more unwieldy and his brain smaller (or at least somnolent), so that he became helpless before nimble bodies and wits.

A foretaste was provided at the Battle of Falkirk in 1298, when the English knights, although eventually victorious over the Scots, were at first rendered helpless by a morass which screened the enemy front. Four years later, in the Battle of the Spurs at Courtrai, the French chivalry suffered an appalling defeat at the hands of the Flemish burghers. In order to attack the massed pikemen the French had to cross the Groeninghebeke, where the soft going was enough to throw the first and second lines into confusion; the Flemings had the River Lys to secure their left flank and a swamp on their right. After the battle, at which incidentally no quarter was given, 700 pairs of gilt spurs were recovered from the slain and hung up in the local church. Pikemen and brains had overcome the most powerful weapon of the time. The writing was on the wall, but neither Walter of Brienne nor his allies could read.

Nor, regrettably, had they studied the mystical history of the site, otherwise they would have learned of the great flood of the Boeotian plain in the time of Ogyges, allegedly in 2136 B.C. Frazer points out that Lake Copais depends for its drainage on subterranean passages in the limestone rock; when these are blocked, the plain becomes a marsh.[9] It was the same mechanism which Heracles used when he blocked up the two tunnels built by the Minyans, through which the Kephissos drained, thus flooding the plain of Copais. 'His object was to immobilize the Minyan cavalry.'[10]

But to the Frankish knights the choice of level ground by the

Catalans seemed highly opportune; they did not pause to reflect that they were facing a band of warriors whose tactics were in no way inferior to their courage. In fact, the Catalans had passed the previous days in diverting parts of the River Kephissos through invisible channels among the young grass. They were thus protected in front and at one side by an artificial morass, and on the other by the waters of Lake Copais. Did they perhaps have with them an adventurer who had fought at the Battle of Courtrai nine years before?

It is difficult to decide on the numbers of the contestants; averaging the three versions of the battle (Byzantine, French[11] and the Chronicle of Muntaner) we arrive at a figure for the Franks of 3,000 horse, of whom several hundred were nobles and knights, and 12,000 foot, most of them Greeks recruited from the Duchy of Athens. The Company, on the other hand, numbered 3,000 Spaniards, including 500 cavalry, as well as upwards of 2,000 Turks, Turcopoles and recruited prisoners.[12]

The trysting day named by the Duke of Athens was 10 March 1311 and the place Zituni (Lamia); this is where, on that date, he made his will. It is strange that he had to take his cumbersome force so far from his capital at Thebes, when the enemy was encamped nearer to the latter city. At a guess, it may have been necessary to collect the garrisons he had placed in the castles so recently captured for him by the Catalans; alternatively, he may have assumed that the Company would try to escape from his powerful army and planned to cut the fugitives off from the wild country of Thessaly.

Walter of Brienne and his army followed the present road that runs from Lamia to Livadia (Lebadeia) and presumably took four days to cover the sixty miles that brought him past Chaeronea, where today the huge lion that marked the grave of the Thebans stands by the roadside. It was probably abandoned in the fields at that time, but had it stood on its pedestal Walter would have taken it as a favourable omen, for his own standard sported a golden lion. There, by the stream called Haemon, rises the hill of Thourion, where the Athenians had stood on the fatal day of Chaeronea, before 'that dishonest victory, fatal to liberty', as Milton was to call it. On this hill Walter too is said to have stood, surveying the battle ground, before descending to lead his picked nobles and knights against the pitiful remains of the Catalan Company.

For pitiful they seemed, when the Turks and Turcopoles had left their ranks and stationed themselves away from the battlefield. They could not believe that the Duke of Athens could be so un-grateful and so forgetful of their services that he wished to destroy the men of the Catalan Company. In their simple minds, now be-coming experienced in western perfidy, arose the suspicion that the preparations for battle were merely a sham and that the Franks and Catalans had made a secret pact to murder them. Thus there re-mained less than 4,000 Catalans, most of them without defensive armour. Pitiful indeed.

But they had some compensation from an unexpected change on the Franco-Greek side. The 200 horse and 300 infantry whom the duke had retained when he dismissed the Company came to their employer and, in Muntaner's words, said, 'Lord, our brothers are here, whom we see you wish to destroy, a great wrong and a great sin, wherefore we leave you, for we want to go and die with them; and so we defy you and take our leave of you'.[13] The duke, contemp-tuous as ever, felt that he could well do without them and dismissed them with the remark that they could go to the devil, for it was just as well that they should die with the others.

So they went and joined their comrades. I called them pitiful, but note that the word applies only to their numbers and outward show. There were no gaudy pennants, no golden spurs nor silver trumpets. But the backbone was still the old Almugavar, who had been fighting the French for twenty-five years; first French Philip III in Catalonia, then Charles of Anjou and his son in Sicily and Calabria. A few there must have been who had fought and plun-dered their way from the Pyrenees to the Taurus Mountains; standing shoulder to shoulder with them were their sons, born in the camps of Sicily and Tunis, veterans already of the campaigns against Turks and Greeks. Their weapons and clothing were the same as ever; the silks and ornaments they had won had no place on the battlefield. They were still the most powerful and most accurate marksmen with their javelins, the boldest in attack, the staunchest in defence, the fiercest and most agile, the finest infantry in the world.

It was Monday 15 March. The day was sunny and the light danced on the brilliant armour, the gilt spurs and the jewelled sword belts of 700 nobles and knights. It played on the vivid colours of emblazoned surcoats, caparisons and shields, on pennants and plumes and the lion banner of Brienne. Walter placed himself ahead of the front rank, his standard bearer by his side, as they walked and then trotted towards the silent Catalans. At the sudden, stern shout of *'Aragó! Aragó!'* some of the horses swerved towards the lake; they were checked and, though less neatly mustered, all moved forward again.

With the Catalans silent again the armoured lines advanced until but an arrow flight separated them from the enemy. Then from the visored helmets came the war cries, *'Montjoie!'* and *'St Denis!'* as the riders set spurs to their steeds and vied with each other to be first among the Catalans. With lances couched and shields held high, with loose rein and bloody spur, they launched themselves at the narrow strip of meadow that remained.

It was Courtrai over again. Each knight, as he felt his horse sinking, urged it forward in the belief that he was crossing a marshy rivulet; at every step he confidently expected firmer ground and at every step his horse sank deeper into the mire. The Catalans were all but within their reach and it seemed impossible that they should not be able to cross the narrow gap. The second line, seeing the first immobile, spurred forward to their aid and found itself too sinking into the morass. Retreat and advance alike became impossible for the huddled horsemen in their iron carapaces. Horses slipped and fell, men floundered in the mud and neither rose again. Others stood like statues, caught fast in the grip of the swamp, horse and rider sinking imperceptibly.

At the height of the confusion and when all the enemy cavalry had entered the fatal area, the Almugavars hurled their javelins into the seething mass. I have said that they were the world's best marksmen, steady, strong and deliberate, so that each shaft found its mark. Then they drew their short swords, the dreaded *coltell catalanesc*, and plunged in among the survivors. The Duke of Athens had been among the first to die and as he fell from his horse, so did the lion banner fall in the bloody mire. Now the shouts of *'Montjoie!'* and *'St Denis!'* wavered and died away and the shouts of *'Aragó!'* and *'Sant Jordi!'* grew ever stronger. The Turcopoles and Turks, convinced by now that this was no staged ruse, rushed to join the massacre, and later one of them was seen parading Walter of Brienne's head on a spear. And while this was taking place, the Company's cavalry were in among the unprotected infantry, killing and maiming with every stroke.

But it was the nobles and knights who drained the bitter cup. Alas for their pomp and panoply! Alas for gallant men and willing steeds! Methodically they were done to death, the cavaliers who had so blithely spurred into action. Of the 200 who had used their gilt spurs to reach their doom more quickly, and the 400 or 500 who followed them, only four or five survived. Bonifacio of Verona was one, spared because of his fair dealing with the Company, and Roger Deslaur of Roussillon, a fellow Catalan and former envoy of the duke. Though the chroniclers give these as the only survivors we know from other sources, according to Miller, that Jean de Maisy of Euboea escaped, perhaps because he had treated the captive Ferdinand with courtesy, as did the eldest son of the Duke of Naxos, later to marry the Jeannette to whose hand Rocafort had aspired. The Lord of Carditza lived to build a church near Lake Copais, as an inscription shows, perhaps as a thank-offering for his survival.

Other than these the Frankish chivalry had perished. Albert Pallavicini, Thomas de Stromoncourt, Reginald de la Roche, George Ghisi, these were among the greatest. But throughout mainland Greece, Achaia and the islands, families mourned their dead. So great was the slaughter of the fatal day of Kephissos that Theodulos Magister solemnly stated that not even an army chaplain escaped.

It was the end of a hundred years' domination of a foreign land and on that Monday in March an entire civilization began to crumble. Apart from castles it has bequeathed us little: an occasional *tournois*[14] is still thrown up by the plough, seals and documents survive in museums, but of human traces there are none. After a century the Franks were still a foreign garrison and a happy blend, such as that of Norman and Anglo-Saxon, was not even attempted. So ended a grandiose dominion, won by fraud, sustained by force and brought down by pride.

The methodical slaughter of helpless men no longer shocks students of medieval history. It was the avowed aim of Walter of Brienne and it was the Company's usual policy. As long as there was a chance of a prisoner causing harm, he was better dead; a conqueror had indeed to be confident of his strength to allow his followers the luxury of taking prisoners for ransom. Death solved all problems. So it was at Courtrai and so it would be at Crecy; only at Bannockburn, fought three years later with similar tactics, did the thrifty Scots take live prisoners for ransom, and then only those of blood and coat armour.

The Battle of the Kephissos was a warning that the warfare of massed cavalry attacks had passed its peak. Well-placed infantry, with well-directed missiles, whether arrows or spears, proved superior to the heavily-armoured knights who, even while their tactics were obsolescent, were wearing ever more elaborate and heavy suits of plate, and riding larger and less manœuvrable chargers. They were to believe in their own invincibility for another two centuries, until gunpowder laid them low; but then the dinosaurs took a million years to be found out.

Epilogue
1311–88

The situation of the Catalans after the Battle of the Kephissos may be compared with that of a man who wins a lottery in which he has not taken a ticket. The change from freebooter to landowner, from outlaw to lawgiver, was a profound one; that it should happen in the space of a few hours, unprecedented. How would the Almugavars change destruction for construction? The rise and fall of a colony is a less theatrical story than what has gone before; nevertheless the tale has its own interest and must be told.

The news of the disaster at Kephissos came as a stunning blow to the rest of Greece, though it made no lasting impression elsewhere. Today its memory, like that of other decisive battles,* lingers in the mind of a few scholars and, till recently, in folk memory round Lake Copais. The victory was so overwhelming that the thought of reversing it seems not even to have been entertained; the apathetic Greek population saw a change of masters which did not seem prejudicial to them. On the night of the battle the Catalans occupied the camp of the defeated Franks and on the next day marched to Livadia, a strongly fortified and prosperous city. In spite of its being the favourite property of the Brienne family the Greeks immediately opened its gates to the victorious Company and in return were awarded full privileges as new members under its great seal. Elsewhere the Greeks either passively accepted their change of masters

---

* How many readers could identify the victories of Zama, Wadi Bedr, Hattin and Navas de Tolosa?

or fled with their possessions to the Venetian stronghold of Negroponte. Then Thebes was sacked and occupied (the famous castle
was not destroyed at this time, as often stated) and the Company
went on to Athens, which surrendered without resistance. This
alone gives us an indication of the tenuous hold of the Franks over
their Greek possessions.

For a period of three generations the Catalan Grand Company
and its descendants were to live as a settled community, heirs to the
feudal system of the Burgundian dukes. Here at last was the new
home which the Catalan Company had been seeking since it left
Sicily. Not a warrior was left to resist them as they apportioned the
fiefs. The widows of Kephissos became the wives of the victors, the
bluest blood being apportioned to the toughest fighter. Many an
Almugavar lorded it as the husband of some noble lady 'whose
wash-handbasin', in Muntaner's words, 'he was not worthy to
hold'. A bitter fate for many a dame who had grown up in the artificial surrounds of the Theban court, where troubadours sang of
knightly deeds, where they had coyly bestowed a scarf on a favoured
knight or sat in judgment at the Court of Love. The Catalans kept
their own language as the official one, but found it expedient to
employ Greeks as scribes and notaries, probably because they
themselves were illiterate. The Greeks prospered moderately and
one infers that they were treated more like human beings; two of
their notaries were later elected to the governing council and the
Greek population, ignored in Frankish archives for a century, comes
to life again in the annals of the Catalans.

The Company's most pressing need was a leader. Hostile nations
crowded at every frontier. The Venetians threatened them from
Negroponte, across the narrow strait; the remaining Franks would
soon begin to think of revenge; the Greeks of Thessaly and Epiros,
supported for the moment by the Emperors of Byzantium in virtue
of a tripartite alliance, were ready to invade from the north and
west; and the Genoese would never forget the injuries they had
sustained at the Almugavars' hands.

Of the nobles and knights who had shared their campaigns not
one had survived and they had to look elsewhere for a chief, and
quickly at that. Their dilemma did not conflict with their democratic principles; they knew that no western nation would contemplate diplomatic relations with anyone less than a gentleman, so a
gentleman they must have. They solved the immediate problem in a

manner typical of the Company's fantastic history and with its usual good fortune. They offered the command to one of the two prisoners they had taken at the Kephissos, Bonifacio de Verona. We have met him before and know him for an honourable knight; but he dared not prejudice his position with the Venetians, for his principal estates lay next to their territory in Negroponte. On his refusal the Catalans settled for the other prisoner, their compatriot Roger Deslaur. He accepted the offer, which included the great castle of Salona, lately the property of the last Thomas de Stromoncourt, and the hand of the newly made widow, which went with the seigniory.

Having thus achieved a measure of respectability they sent envoys to Frederick of Sicily,[1] expressing the wish to be under his rule and praying him to send one of his sons to be their overlord. He nominated his second legitimate son, Manfred, who was still a child (see Table 4); as Manfred's deputy, and entitled to receive their homage, Frederick sent a Catalan knight of Ampurias, Berenguer Estañol, who arrived in 1312 and allowed Deslaur to retire to his new fief of Salona.

Estañol's first task was to defeat enemies on every side. The Pope had excommunicated the Catalan Company and made a martyr of

Table 4

The Aragonese Dukes of Athens

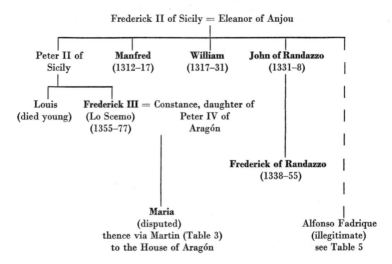

Frederick II of Sicily = Eleanor of Anjou

Peter II of Sicily | Manfred (1312–17) | William (1317–31) | John of Randazzo (1331–8)

Louis (died young) | Frederick III (Lo Scemo) (1355–77) = Constance, daughter of Peter IV of Aragón

Frederick of Randazzo (1338–55)

Maria (disputed) thence via Martin (Table 3) to the House of Aragón

Alfonso Fadrique (illegitimate) see Table 5

the late Walter of Brienne, whom they had regarded as a welsher; he referred to him as a 'true athlete of Christ and true boxer of the Church'[2] and called for a Crusade. None was forthcoming and Estañol was thus able to lead his Almugavars against his hostile neighbours and defeat them piecemeal.

The Catalans next set about forming a constitution. It developed gradually but in all essentials it followed the democratic principles already laid down in Catalonia; documents of the next sixty years make it quite clear that the 'universities' (i.e. the municipalities) were constituted according to, and would continue to enjoy, 'the statutes, constitution, usages and customs of Barcelona'. This applied of course, only to the conquerors and such others as had been admitted to citizenship.[3]

There was necessarily a parliament, one of Spain's oldest institutions, whose memory we saw in the Council of Twelve during the wandering years; it was composed of *síndics*, or representatives, of each town in the duchy. As executive officers there were a vicar-general (civil) and a marshal (military); the posts were later combined. These are merely the outlines of a system under which feudalism and democracy existed side by side in apparent harmony. Local government followed the same lines, with municipalities very conscious of their rights and sturdily prepared to uphold them, even against the duke.

The Catalans of course maintained the Roman Catholic religion as introduced by the Crusaders, in spite of being excommunicated from time to time. They preserved the archbishoprics of Athens and Thebes and added one at Zituni as soon as they acquired the territory of Neopatras. While the ducal court (without the absentee duke) continued to reside at Thebes, where the magnificent castle of St Omer provided more comfort than the cramped quarters in the propylaea of the Acropolis, Athens remained the important religious centre. The Parthenon had for eight centuries been dedicated to the worship of a Virgin greater than Athene and now became *La Seu* (the cathedral) *de Santa Maria*, situated in the *Castell de Cetines*, by which name the Acropolis was now known. The Greek Orthodox Church, meanwhile, continued to occupy the inferior position it had filled under the Burgundian dukes.

But in spite of royal and ducal patronage, a democratic government and three archbishops, the duchy became poorer as time went on: by 1340 Athens was a decaying town, compared with Thebes, and towards the end of their rule the Catalans of Athens were complaining to the duke of their poverty and distress. In existing documents, in fact the city of Athens is not even mentioned between 1350 and 1370. In Thebes too there is less and less evidence of the rich textile industry which was at once the pride and support of the splendid ducal city under the Burgundians. It may be more than coincidence that the manufacture of textiles has for centuries been a staple industry of Catalonia; thus in 1444 a cloth hall was built for English and other customers, who brought their wool to Barcelona to be woven. Is it not possible that many of the industrious weavers of Thebes were taken to Spain during the time of the Catalan occupation, just as the Norman kingdom of Sicily removed their ancestors 200 years earlier?

Another factor was the ill-advised treaty made with Venice in 1319, which had the effect of crippling the duchy's seaborne trade while it protected the Venetians from piratical Almugavar raids on their Aegean possession. The only functions of the new duchy were to provide an outlet for the trade of Barcelona and Mallorca and to act as a base for trading ventures further from home. When it lost these poverty became inevitable. The tenuous life and inexorable death of the Catalan duchy can best be deduced from the *Carta Catalana*, the commercial map of oriental trade drawn in 1375 by the Mallorcan Jew Abraham Cresques. From this it is plain that the main trade routes to the east passed either through Damascus and Syrian ports, or through Alexandria and Cairo, while the northerly route through the Black Sea called for free passage along the Bosphorus, not readily granted by their old enemies the Genoese. Athens and Thebes were thus commercial backwaters. Their value was merely one of prestige, too small to warrant the expenditure of men or money for their defence. This is why, during the whole life of the duchy, a single reinforcement was sent for the defence of the Acropolis—twelve men-at-arms.

Berenguer Estañol fell ill and died and in 1316 the Council sent to Sicily to ask for a replacement. Manfred died in November of 1317 and his father now nominated his next son, William, as duke; but this did not solve the difficulty of finding a suitable regent. Fortunately, King Frederick decided on an intelligent, if illegitimate, son, Alfonso Fadrique* de Aragón.

* In view of the number of Fredericks who obtrude, I have kept the form Fadrique to distinguish this important character.

The Catalan Company received him joyously and rightly looked forward to happy years under his vicariate. One of the first, wisest and no doubt pleasantest acts of the new regent was to marry Marulla, daughter of Bonifacio da Verona. She was both pretty and sensible and Muntaner, who was detained in her father's house when she was a girl of eight (see chapter 8), was much taken with her. Marulla was Bonifacio's principal heiress; on her mother's side she was equally well dowered with a third of Negroponte and important interests in the Morea. In this way Alfonso Fadrique got a firm grip on the large estates in Attica that Guy de la Roche had bestowed on Bonifacio at his coming-of-age ceremony (see chapter 10). So advantageous, in fact, was the marriage that the Venetians, who owned the greater part of Negroponte, were justified in viewing the Catalan-Lombard alliance with misgivings.

Since the Company had taken over the duchy of Athens the Venetians had in any case felt insecure. Raids across the narrow channel that separates Attica and Negroponte were frequent and to counter them the Venetians had been forced to maintain a defensive squadron. It is noteworthy that Bonifacio had refused to contribute to the expense entailed, thus revealing, not only his Catalan sympathies, but his immunity from the raiders.

Alfonso Fadrique combined personal attractions with all the better qualities of the royal house of Aragón. He was shrewd and far-seeing, but by no means averse to making a bold move when the opportunity presented itself. With his arrival the Catalan threat to neighbouring nations became organized and large territories in the north were conquered; the annexation of much of Thessaly and the death of the sebastokrator John allowed the second ducal title of Neopatras (or Neopatria) to be incorporated with that of Athens.

The time was now ripe for the resumption of Catalan commercial relations with the Byzantines, and a pact was made with the businessmen of Barcelona, who negotiated an agreement with the Emperor Andronicus. The treaty disposed for the moment of one potential enemy, though a distant one. The Venetians of Negroponte, however, were nearer and less tractable. They were businessmen with the modest ambition of acquiring all the trade of the Levant. They were also smarting under the Catalans' refusal to allow their Roman Catholic bishop to return to his see in Negroponte, presumably because he was a member of the House of Brienne. An absence of more than three months could lead to loss of his bishoprie. Alfonso

Fadrique determined to try the effect of a show of force; at the same time he was probing the reception he was likely to have when he claimed the inheritance of his wife.

In 1318 he crossed the bridge at Chalkis with a mixed force that included Turkish mercenaries and invaded the Lombard and Venetian possessions. Many of their owners had perished at the Battle of the Kephissos and little opposition was met. So readily, in fact, did the local landowners accept peace terms that the whole of Negroponte seemed fruit ripe for the plucking; to encourage the Catalans further, the death of Bonifacio enabled Alfonso Fadrique, his son-in-law, to occupy the castles of Karystos and Larmena, which had been part of Marulla's inheritance.

But these too rapid successes alarmed neighbours who feared an upset in the balance of power. The Angevins, hardened meddlers in Greece, raised an outcry; the Briennes began hungering for a return to Athens and feared for the few possessions they had retained in the Morea. And wherever the Angevins meddled the Pope was sure to prepare his supporting artillery, the anathema. In this instance he criticized the employment of heathen Turkish mercenaries in a dispute among Christian states, and encouraged the Venetians to drive out 'the offscourings of humanity'. The horror expressed at the employment of Turks was hypocritical; the Catalans' action had numerous precedents: the Byzantine Greeks (who were possibly not counted as Christians) employed Turkish mercenaries constantly from 1259 onwards (see chapter 6, note 9); there are records of Turkish troops fighting for the Frankish descendants of the crusaders in 1263 and 1283, and of Saracens in the Angevin ranks at the same time. But memory can be conveniently short and the accusation of using Turkish allies could be relied on to arouse antipathy.

Bowing to the storm King Frederick of Sicily advised Alfonso Fadrique to sign a truce with the Venetians.[4] All that the Catalans got out of it was Venetian neutrality while they enlarged their holdings on the mainland, and the possible advantage of being on good terms with Genoa's chief rival. In return they undertook to give no help to the Catalan pirates who had become a menace in the Aegean. The treaty further stipulated that the Catalans would fit out no more vessels on the coasts of Attica, though they were still permitted to maintain a fleet in the Gulf of Corinth. Such Catalan ships as were in Athenian harbours at the time of signing the treaty were each to have a plank removed from the hull and their loose gear was to be stored in the castle of Cetines (the Acropolis).

The long period of Catalan rule over the duchies of Athens and Neopatras is usually passed over lightly by all but specialists in the history of Hispano-Levantine relations. We are told, with little evidence, that the Almugavars lapsed into a prolonged debauch and forgot their former mastery over the art of war.[5] It is true that the lungs which launched the stern '*Aragó!*' and '*Desperta ferre!*' now coaxed flame from damp wood on the hearths of Attica, and that swords once beaten into ploughshares can with difficulty be restored to their former state. But of evidence that the Almugavars lived in slothful ease, I have found no trace.

In fact, while the generation that amazed the Greek world remained, Catalan possessions were steadily expanded and staunchly defended. Under the inspired leadership of Alfonso Fadrique the duchies reached their zenith; when he retired in 1330 the old generation of fighters, whose shoulders had held the sky suspended, were passing away. Their successors saw round them new enemies added to the old, with equally greedy eyes. Nevertheless the successors of the Almugavars, whom we are supposed to regard as a set of incompetent drunkards, kept their duchy for another half century, with little material help from their nominal rulers in the west.

Among recorded episodes we read the following: the Angevins tried once more to push their claim to the Morea and, by borrowing the necessary funds from the Acciajuolis of Florence, gave the latter family a foothold in Greece.

Then young Walter of Brienne, whose mother had taken him away after the Battle of the Kephissos, was of age and eager to recover what he had been taught to think of as his country. He was an Angevin vassal through being Count of Lecce in Italy and, to make sure of their support in the east, had married into the House of Anjou. Pope John XXII was as francophile as his predecessors and opened the campaign with a letter to the archbishops of Patras and Corinth, urging a crusade against the 'sons of iniquity' *(iniquitatis filii)*; in a bull of excommunication he had already thundered against the 'schismatic sons of perdition and foster-children of iniquity' *(scismatici perditionis filii et iniquitatis alumni . . .)* who had expelled Duke Walter and continued to occupy his duchy. Thus fortified by ghostly support and pawning his wife's dowry for ready

143

money, Walter enlisted a force of 800 French knights and as many or more Italian soldiers. To his disappointment the Venetians, on whom he had been counting for help from Negroponte, had again renewed their truce with the Catalans.[6]

Walter began, in Crusading style, by attacking and conquering places that had no connection with the Catalans; but when he came up against their territory he met with one disappointment after another. At the Kephissos the homeless Company had achieved a brilliant victory by its tactics in the open. If Walter, as optimistic and hot-headed as his late father, hoped to repeat the encounter with due care to avoid swamps, he was to be baulked. The Catalans were now defending a homeland; all they had to do was to stay in their castles and walled towns and let time do the rest. The Greek population, which had confidently been expected to rise against their new masters, found these no worse than their previous ones; they raised not a finger to help restore what a contemporary, perhaps with his tongue in his cheek, called 'their ancient happiness'. It was now Walter's turn to learn what the Catalans had taught their previous employers: 'no money, no fight', and in the following year he had to take his army back home. It would be twenty-five years until he was killed at Poitiers by the Black Prince.

The only permanent result of the Crusade was the sad loss of the castle of St Omer at Thebes. One of the great achievements of the age, in architecture and decoration, it was too dangerous for the Catalans to leave in the hands of an ally. Rather than risk its betrayal to an enemy, they destroyed it methodically, gaining another bad mark in the history books. But we should remember that those who deplored the destruction of the castle looked on unmoved when ancient columns and sculptures were used as building blocks in their houses, or consigned to the lime-burner. We detect more than the outraged artist when the chronicler writes, 'Behold the barbarity which the vile Catalans [in some versions 'dogs of Catalans'] wrought in destroying such a castle and such a great fortress.'[7]

The excommunication in support of Walter of Brienne had an unexpected and welcome result, for it provides us with a nominal roll of the upper crust of the Catalan Company at the time. Pope Benedict was running no risks of the bolts of Heaven falling on the wrong heads and therefore supplied the divine vengeance with names and addresses. This also ensured that no deserving character was left undamned. We notice ample signs of foreign dilution among the original Spanish names, and French ones such as Adelin, Minoy, Traine and La Lièvre are prominent.

The Pope's representative on the spot had a better idea of Greek affairs; Archbishop Isnard of Thebes, sensing that his flock might be pushed over to the Orthodox 'heresy', celebrated mass before a Catalan congregation in the cathedral.[8] So much for anathema. But he went further. On his own responsibility he cancelled the sentence of excommunication and, through the Latin patriarch of Constantinople, managed to make the Pope change his mind and receive Catalan envoys. The reconciliation was effected in 1343 by his successor, Clement VI, who overrode Walter of Brienne's objections and welcomed the Catalans, a buffer state between the Turks and the west, back into the fold.[9]

During the latter years of the 1330s the Company had to turn its attention to the Serbians and Albanians, who were infiltrating into Thessaly. The absentee dukes were dying off in Sicily (see Table 4) and with the death of Alfonso Fadrique faded any hopes of survival that the duchies might have entertained. Members of his family continued to figure in the records, usually occupying important posts and in one case celebrated in legend;[10] but could do no more than postpone the inevitable collapse.

Whatever may be alleged of the loss of warlike spirit among the Catalans of Athens, the nation was still sound and enterprising. What one senses is a lack of purpose; they were ready to march and to fight, but none seemed to know whither or against whom. When John Cantacuzene was disputing the throne of Byzantium he made use of many Athenian Catalan mercenaries, even in the imperial guard; his high opinion of their valour and warlike temperament is evident in his autobiography.[11] Their loyalty was never in question, which makes us believe that the enmity between the original Catalan Company and Andronicus II was not wholly the former's fault.

As the Sicilian Aragonese rulers grew ever more feeble—Frederick *lo Scemo* ('The Fool', see Table 4) is a fair example—Peter IV of Aragón began considering how he could win their territories for his crown. He evinced increasing interest in the duchies of Athens and Neopatras. Even while Frederick Randazzo was still alive and nominally Duke of Athens, Peter wrote direct to the Catalans in the duchies, calling them 'our countrymen', thanking them for their loyalty to the crown and expressing his pleasure at their great love. And so, at long last, he cancelled the fifty-year-old ban that had caused the Company to go east in 1302.

The middle period of Catalan rule in Athens was clouded by internal disputes, culminating in the murder of an extortionate deputy vicar-general by aggrieved aristocrats. Chief of these was one Roger de Lluria, distantly related to the famous admiral of that name. He had one blot on his record: in 1363, while governor of Thebes, he had called in the Turks as allies against the Venetians as well as against fellow Catalans with whom he had quarrelled. Oblivious of the fact that their parents had earned excommunication for doing the same thing, the Catalans of Athens protested to their Duke in Sicily.

This time there was unanimity. The Pope, the barons of Achaia, the Emperor of Byzantium, the knights of St John and the Athenians

Table 5

The family of Alfonso Fadrique de Aragón

(Lords of Aegina in capitals)

ALFONSO FADRIQUE = Marulla dalle Carceri, daughter of
DE ARAGÓN   Bonifacio di Verona
(d. 1338)

PETER	JAMES FREDERICK	BONIFACIO	William	John
Lord of Salona and Lidorikion	Vicar-general, 1356–65 Inherited Salona, Lidorikion and Aegina. Gave last to younger brother, Bonifacio	d. 1374 Lord of Karystos and Zituni		

Helena Cantacuzene = LUIS
      d. 1382
Took Aegina from his
cousin Peter in 1379.
'The last Count of
Salona' Vicar-general
1376–81

PETER	JOHN	Bonifacio
dispossessed by Luis in 1379	inherited from Luis in 1382 d. 1385	

Maria
(killed by Turks)

ANTONELLO CAOPENA = One daughter, d. 1451

Their descendants, and eventually
ceded to Venice, who
held it alternately with the
Turks

combined. They found the Turkish fleet off Megara[12] and annihilated it; having lost his Asiatic allies Roger now had to hurry to appease the Venetians. How he did this is not stated, but an episode which Miller dates to 1365[13] (Rubió i Lluch to 1359[14]) may be relevant. I have wondered why Bonifacio, third son of Alfonso Fadrique (see Table 5), should have sold the important castles of Larmena and Karystos, his mother's inheritance, to the Venetians for the small sum of 6,000 ducats, serfs and all. Was it part of Roger's policy of appeasement? The transaction of course weakened the duchies still more.

The Catalans were now so short of talent that Roger de Lluria was soon appointed vicar-general in addition to his post of marshal; with supreme power in his hands he guided the erratic destinies of the duchies until his death in 1370. There was nothing strange about changing allies and enemies in those days (is there now?) and Lluria became the foe of the Turks, earning fulsome praise four years after inviting them. But the Venetians, even after appeasement, did not readily overlook Roger's part in the Turkish influx. Though the Catalans would now have liked a proper peace treaty they could obtain no more than a renewal of the fifty-year-old truce. And in spite of protests and prayers, the Venetians still refused to relax the clause prohibiting the Catalans from basing ships in the Saronic Gulf.

It is doubtful whether the Catalans appreciated the importance of a small transaction that took place in 1365; in retrospect it is difficult to over-estimate its importance. Nerio Acciajuoli, cousin and adopted son of Niccolò, was nominated governor of Corinth by the Angevins. One feels that the move was planned by the Italians, for there is something inevitable about the deliberate, stepwise progress of the Florentine family, moving nearer to Athens with every acquisition.

The death of Roger de Lluria (1370), 'in whose veins seethed the blood of the Almugavars',[15] introduced a more chaotic period, of which the Catalans' enemies tried to make use. They marched on Athens, took the city with little effort and then found the Castell de Cetines—the Acropolis—too well defended.

On the death of Frederick the Feeble in 1377, the ambitions of Peter IV of Aragón accorded with the wishes of the Athenian Catalans. He deserves to be remembered, in this bald and factual account, as the only ruler who showed enthusiasm for the glories of classical Greece. An enigmatic king, he is generally known by the nickname *El Ceremonioso*; his Catalan sobriquet, *punyalet* (little dagger) may be more pertinent. Of the Acropolis, which he had not seen, he remarked enthusiastically that it was the richest jewel in the world, which could scarcely be equalled among the kingdoms of Christendom. But he never sent the money that was so badly needed and his military aid was negligible. The sole recorded transaction, in fact, worked the other way, for in 1359 he asked Athens to send him twenty-five Turkish archers.

The beginning of the end occurred in 1374, when Nerio Acciajuoli seized Megara on the slightest of pretexts and established himself within striking distance of Thebes and Athens. He soon found an excellent weapon in one of the bands of mercenaries that was infesting Europe at the time, the Navarrese Company.[16] Anarchy ruled once more throughout the duchies and the distracted inhabitants fled, either to Athens or Negroponte, as did the Frankish subjects over sixty years before. The Venetian duke of the Archipelago joined in the attack on the Catalans; it is probable that there was a last attempt by the Brienne heirs to regain their old duchy, and the Knights of St John, under the mastership of the Aragonese Juan Fernándex d'Heredia,[17] joined in the ravaging of the Catalan possessions.

In Athens, nobly and successfully defended by a handful of Catalans and Greeks, the names of Romeo de Bellarbe and Dimitri Rendi stand out. The community, once the siege had been raised, sent a series of petitions, or 'capitulations', to Peter of Aragón. The important item was a request that the duchies might be joined in perpetuity to the crown of Aragón; it was granted and on 1 September 1380 envoys did homage to Peter as their duke. The title, as distinct from the territory, remained with the House of Aragón for many years; it passed to the united kingdom of Spain when Ferdinand, already married to Isabel of Castile, inherited the throne of Aragón. In this way the kings of Spain came to bear the title 'Duke of Athens and Neopatras' until the end of the seventeenth century, then the Hapsburg dynasty died out.

For a few years the Catalans again tasted peace, with much of their lost territory restored. A strong vicar-general, Rocaberti, came and went. The only figure of note to be left in the duchy was Peter de Pau. His name means 'peace' and he was to belie it. But our attention must not be monopolized by the Catalans, nor must we

> '. . . count for nought
> What the Greek did and what the Florentine'.

Nerio Acciajuoli had bided his time. In 1385, from Megara on the border of Catalan territory, he saw a duchy without duke or vicar-general, without effective troops and, above all, without the fighting spirit of the old Almugavars. He collected mercenaries, horse and foot, Greek and Albanian. He even overcame Venetian objections to foreign warships by keeping a galley for the ostensible purpose of protecting the isthmus of Corinth from Turkish corsairs; these he was in any case sheltering in Megara and he was to use their services later.

The final attack was as subtly and deliberately prepared as his other measures and a woman was selected as the excuse. Maria, heiress to the County of Salona and last representative of the descendants of Alfonso Fadrique, had been for a time engaged to Rocaberti's son. When the marriage was called off Nerio offered his brother-in-law, Pietro Saraceno of Negroponte, as a replacement. The girl's mother was Helena Cantacuzene, descendant of a Byzantine emperor. She was conscious of her blue blood and that her daughter was doubly royal, even if the paternal contribution was through the bastard line of Alfonso Fadrique. The idea of a trades-man as son-in-law is unpleasant to the poor aristocrat and abhorrent to the rich. Helena was rich. She engaged her daughter to Stephen Doukas, a royal Serbian. If Nerio was annoyed he concealed the fact; he had the excuse he needed, a slight by the Catalans. With horse and foot he invaded their lands, left the castle severely alone and marched on Athens.

The lower city was, as usual, overcome without difficulty, but the Acropolis was a tougher proposition. Assisted by Turkish pirates from the Peiraeus (and earning no anathema thereby) Nerio in-vested the fortress and pressed attacks by day and night. For fifteen months Peter de Pau, its stubborn and heroic governor, defended the Castle of Cetines with a handful of men, while repeated mes-sages were sent to John I, the new king of Aragón. More concerned with his domestic problems, the latter was in no hurry to send relief; then leisurely preparations were made for reinforcements to be sent under Rocaberti. But by the time he was ready to sail the garrison of the Acropolis, famished and exhausted, had surrendered to Nerio Acciajuoli. Peter de Pau, the last Almugavar of Greece, as

he has been happily named, had sustained the high renown of the
Catalan Company. On 2 May 1388, the four pales ceased to flutter
over the castle of Athens but the valour of its defenders still arouses
pride in Catalan hearts.

So our tale ends with Florentine merchants as dukes of Athens, a
few soiled relics of the splendid Frankish chivalry surviving in the
Morea and the Ottoman Turks firmly established in Europe. How
different from those days of uninterrupted triumph, when Roger de
Flor led his handful of fighters from one victory to the next, from
the Bosphorus to the Iron Gates of Cilicia! The matchless generation that made Byzantium tremble and destroyed in a day the
world's finest cavalry, what did it accomplish?

In barbarity, destructiveness and lack of pity the Company
equalled the Crusaders; in valour and tactics it occasionally sur-
passed them. Yet the spirit of the Crusades still has the power to fire
the imagination, however brutish its agents may have been. But the
Catalan Grand Company, though it may arouse admiration for its
incomparable bravery and for the fortitude of its men and women,
leaves us with the feeling that it was all to little purpose.

We marvel at their achievements but we judge them by their
works. A few doubtful stretches of masonry in the wall of the
Acropolis or the castles that once sheltered Catalan rulers are the
only monuments that have been ascribed to them. A painting of the
Virgin, now in the Byzantine Museum of Athens, has been called
the *Panaghia catalana* since its discovery in 1849, but is now known
to be of Italian inspiration.[18]

Their memory still persists in those parts that lay under the
heavy hand of the Catalan Vengeance, but it is a sinister one. Old
men from Thrace remember hearing 'May the Catalan vengeance
overtake you!'; in the last century 'Not even a Catalan would do
such a thing' (αὐτὸ οὔτε οἱ καταλάνοι τό κάμνουν) was a common
phrase, while 'What a brute!' was expressed as 'What a Catalan!'
(Διντί καταλάνο) by the old women of Attica. In the Peloponnese an
ugly virago was called a '*catalana*', in contrast to the strong but
beautiful '*amazona*'. Yet in a few remote parts, significantly those
where the Catalans had not penetrated, the name lost its evil conno-
tation and retained only the suggestion of power. In Mani they told
of the peasant returning from a journey and learning that his newly
born son had been christened Peter. Ignorant of the great apostle,

and knowing only that the word meant 'rock', he demanded that it be changed to a more usual one, 'Gerarkarios' or 'Catalanos'.

The cruelty of the Catalans is an accusation which should be examined. They were rapacious and, at the beginning of their adventures, behaved like any other Free Company of the time. Then came the Catalan Vengeance, a typical reaction of any un-civilized people that has been cheated and betrayed. Equal barbari-ties were perpetrated under the banner of the Cross. This does not excuse them and is rightly abhorred in the western so-called civiliza-tion of today, but it might have passed unremarked thirty years ago. Many equally abominable massacres have taken place since their day and are possibly still being perpetrated. No apologist can excuse their conduct, but we can explain it.

In a few instances they helped to shape history. We read that in 1308 the Knights Hospitallers of St John moved their headquarters to the Island of Rhodes; this they would never have done if the Company had not cleared the Turks from the adjacent mainland. But their main achievement was hardly to the advantage of the west; the Company's attack on the treacherous Byzantines was the most formidable that their long-suffering empire had yet sustained; its effects persisted and undoubtedly contributed to the fall of the last Christian bulwark in the near east. And how did they replace the splendid feudal system that perished at the Kephissos? Only by another that became progressively poorer. The capitulations of Athens of 1380, presented by the Council to Peter IV, mention the poverty and burden *(pobretat a afany)* of the inhabitants. The com-mercial success of the Catalans did not extend to the Company; nor, in spite of a few isolated examples, could the duchy claim to be a cultural centre, and occasional foreign references to a university are due to confusion with *universitas,* a community.

However hotly we contend that the farmer and his labourers are the backbone of a country, we know in our hearts that civilization is nurtured, as its name implies, in the city. The seeds may have blown from Galilee or Mecca: the trees were rooted in Rome and Antioch, Damascus and Cordova. The fearless mountaineers of Spain and Roussillon, transported to the archetype of the *polis,* a cradle of civilization, remained country folk; they impoverished themselves and did nothing to enrich the world. They made history and left a vacuum.

How the House of Aragón gained the Throne of Sicily

The Arabs took Sicily from the Byzantines and a handful of obscure Norman adventurers took it from the Arabs. With the inherent genius of the Vikings they not only conquered the island but founded a dynasty of kings from the Hauteville family of Coutances, in Normandy. Adopting the best of the feudal, Byzantine and Norman systems, they built a workable, indeed a prosperous and enlightened kingdom. The last Hauteville king was William II, whose wife, Joanna (daughter of our Henry II), had produced no children. The successor to the kingdom of Sicily was therefore his aunt Constance, who was married to Henry VI Hohenstaufen, Holy Roman Emperor. He had gained the title and his estates from a famous father, the Emperor Barbarossa, drowned during the third Crusade. Henry and Constance produced one child, destined to become greater than either of them.

In the person of Frederick II Hohenstaufen were combined the Holy Roman Empire, at that time a family concern, and the kingdom of Sicily. He is therefore also called Frederick I of Sicily. Of his four wives (the fourth, Bianca Lancia, was his mistress but their offspring were legitimized) two produced children who feature in our tale; the first and third, Constance of Aragón and Isabella of England, are therefore not included in Table 1 (see p. 14).

On the death of Frederick in 1250 the Sicilian kingdom went to Manfred. Urban IV, a Frenchman, saw his opportunity of wreaking papal vengeance on the Hohenstaufens, who had consistently flouted his predecessors. He therefore invited the dour, scheming and vindictive Charles of Anjou to help himself to the kingdom of Sicily, which at that time included southern Italy. Charles was ambitious and had designs on Constantinople; in fact he later confessed that he had accepted the offer of Sicily only as a stepping stone to that object. It was a slippery one. But he had the backing of the next French Pope, Clement IV, and of his own wife, Beatrice, who was mortified at being a mere princess while her younger sisters were queens.

In 1266 Charles of Anjou invaded Italy and defeated and killed Manfred at the Battle of Benevento. The battle was more than a dynastic upheaval. The death of Manfred may have postponed the Renaissance for two centuries; he was one of the great poets of his day (Dante praised his verse) and through his wife he was in touch with Byzantine civilization, which later played an important part in the Great Rebirth.

Charles quickly occupied Sicily and installed an unpopular French garrison. In the following year he concluded the Treaty of Viterbo with the deposed last Latin ruler of Constantinople— Baldwin II. By this he gained the suzerainty of Achaia and infused a tincture of legality into his ambitions.

In 1268 the legitimate Hohenstaufen claimant of the next generation, Conradin, the grandson of Frederick, invaded Italy; he was defeated at Tagliacozzo by Charles of Anjou, or rather by the 500 knights of William of Villehardouin, Prince of Achaia, who were fighting for their new suzerain. Conradin was captured and Charles earned great unpopularity by having him publicly executed in Naples. And this is where the House of Aragón enters the story. As Table 1 shows, Manfred's heir was his daughter Constance, whose claim was upheld by her husband, Peter of Aragón, son and heir apparent of James the Conqueror, Count of Barcelona and King of Aragón. Constance was the next legitimate claimant and seventeen-year-old Conradin, standing on the scaffold awaiting his turn to be beheaded, turned to the crowd and tossed them a glove, with the words, 'This for Peter'.

Fourteen years later Sicily flared up in a spontaneous* revolt and massacre of the French. Fearful of Charles of Anjou's revenge, the

---

* But it is probable that Michael VIII Palaeologos of Byzantium had a hand in the Sicilian Vespers, as the revolt was called, for Charles' fleet at Messina was ready to sail and attack Constantinople.

Sicilians invited Peter of Aragón to rule them. He arrived with his Almugavars and the War of the Vespers began. The people of Sicily had chosen well; Peter the Great, as he is now called, was bold, brilliant and courtly, the rock on which Charles' ambitions were wrecked. Peter died in 1285 and was succeeded by his eldest son, Alfonso III, in Aragón and his fourth child, James, in Sicily. When Alfonso died in 1291 James I of Sicily became his successor in Aragón; in order to appease the Pope he traded Sicily for Corsica and Sardinia. But the Sicilians would have nothing to do with this arrangement and invited the third brother, Frederick, to be their king (see Table 3). This was Frederick II of Sicily (I have consistently called him so to avoid confusion with Frederick II Hohenstaufen, his great-grandfather), often called Frederick the Almugavar. Remarkably, this able and popular king, though at war with the Pope, France, Anjou, Castile and even Aragón, brought the War of the Vespers to a satisfactory conclusion, sealing the treaty with the usual matrimonial alliance. By their support of Frederick against their liege-lord James, the Catalan Company which had conquered Sicily was held to be guilty of treason.

Notes

Prologue

1 Bréhier, *Instituciones,* I, ch. 2 and II, ch. 1.

2 There has been considerable discussion regarding the origin of the word *Almugavar*. Some have derived it from *algaras,* mounted foraging parties; others from *gabar,* fierce, brave; others again from *el-muhavir,* he who brings news, and still others from *maghreb,* the west and especially the north-west of Africa. Many orientalists, however, deny a connection with any Arabic word.

Chapter 1

1 The family of Raoul was French and is believed to persist as the wealthy Rallis and Ralles. They are remembered as leading cotton merchants in Egypt and elsewhere.

2 Pachymeres writes that the Company arrived in the month of Gamelion, in the second indiction. This puts the date in September 1303, instead of 1302. The point does not affect the story.

3 See E. Gibbon, *Decline and Fall of the Roman Empire,* ch. 60.

4 S. Estébanez Calderón, prologue to Cánovas del Castillo, *La Campana de Huesca,* Buenos Aires, Espasa-Calpe Argentine, second edition, 1950, p. 16.

5 Sometimes called *azagaya,* a Berber word adopted by Spanish and Portuguese, through whom South African spears got the name *assegai.*

6 In Estremadura, land of the conquistadores of America, there is still a family named Golfín.

7 Desclot, *Cronica del Rey En Pere,* chs 102, 103.

8 Ibid.

9 Muntaner, *Cronica,* ch. 124.

10 Manzano, *Los Grandes Capitanes Españoles,* p. 28.

11 Schlumberger, *Expédition.*

Chapter 2

1 Nicolau d'Olwer, *L'Expansio*, sect. 29. The name reminds us that, when Charles of Valois proclaimed himself King of Aragón in 1284, the papal legate, for want of a crown, used a hat in the coronation ceremony (Rubió, 'La Companyia', . . . *Miscellanea Prat de la Riba*, p. 230).

2 Pachymeres, *Histoire de Constantinople*, 10.

3 *Or, four pales gules*. Wilfred the Hairy, Count of Barcelona, was severely wounded while fighting for Charles the Bald against the Vikings. When Charles visited him after the battle he asked what reward he would like for his heroism. The wounded man pointed to his plain, gold shield to draw attention to its lack of a device. The king thought for a moment, then said, 'A device won with blood should be inscribed with blood', and, dipping his fingers in the wound that was still oozing over Wilfred's chest, drew them down the shield, thus producing the four bars, or *pales*; these became the emblem of the kingdom of Aragón when the counts of Barcelona became its kings.

4 As an example of the mixed nationalities in the Company, note that Corberán d'Alet was a Navarrese (Rubió, Per que' . . . *Miscellanea Prat de la Riba*, 23).

5 Nicolau d'Olwer, op. cit., sect. 19.

6 The Byzantine Greeks, as heirs to the Roman Empire, described themselves as 'Romans' and all westerners as 'Franks' or 'Latins'. See *Corpus Scriptorum Historiae Byzantinae*, vol. 4, Venice, 1729.

7 Nikephoros Gregoras, for instance, was a child at the time. When he grew up he became a close friend of Andronicus II and used to visit him regularly to console him after his forced abdication. He does not even pretend to be impartial.

8 Moncada, *Expedición*, ch. 12.

Chapter 3

1 Schlumberger, *Expédition*. It is difficult to understand why this route was chosen. The more direct one runs from Akhisar to Alaşehir (Philadelphia) through open country among the imposing Lydian tumuli.

2 There are very few remains of the ancient city since the earthquake of 1968 and none of the old landmarks is recognizable. Even the north wall is now represented by only a few fragments.

3 Midday and not the ninth hour. We have made the same adjustment with the word 'noon'.

4 *Corpus Scriptorum Historiae Byzantinae*, vol. 4, Venice, 1729.

5 A glaring error; the great majority had left after the affair at Cyzicus.

6 Pachymeres relates that after Cyzicus, while taking possession of the Turkish baggage, Roger found some of the soldiers pilfering and had the Bulgarian Cranislas strangled—a Byzantine rather than a western method of execution.

7 Rubió *(Els Catalans a Grècia*, Barcelona, 1937; a small popular work) hints at an intrigue between Roger and his mother-in-law.

8 Kiz Kulesi (Maiden's Tower). It is on the north side of the road from Kemalpaşa to Izmir, an imposing rectangular block, with the window spaces of the first floor intact. The alternate squared blocks of tawny stone and bands of red brick courses are still impressive.

9 The ruins of this theatre, with olive trees carefully preserved as they grow out between the seats, are among the most evocative of the ancient world. It is doubtful whether they would have been uncovered in the fourteenth century.

10 Magnesia ad Meandrum, not the present Manisa near Izmir. Considerable stretches of the wall still stand, showing their rubble core between ashlar facings. There is also a Roman building at the river gate, possibly a gymnasium, and the foundations of a Greek temple among the brambles. The town has been abandoned completely and its deserted remains allow the passage of a high road and a railway line.

11 There is a line of low hills about a mile from Tira, in the plain. It would provide the besiegers' camp with a defence and a look-out post.

12 Kuşadaşi is now a summer resort, with both its castles over-restored. That on the island is now joined to the mainland by a causeway and has a casino, with bar and souvenir shop and, in fact, everything that appeals to the vulgar taste. There is no natural harbour and it is possible that Aonés' ships were beached on the sand during the winter.

13 Homer, *Iliad*, II, 459. My translation.

14 The story of the manna, which goes back to St Augustine, refers to a sandy exudation, which was all that remained of the saint after he ascended in a fiery cloud. Muntaner may have got the story from Voragine's *Golden Legend*, written before 1264, nearly seventy years before Muntaner wrote. (Jacques de Voragine, *La Légende Dorée*, vol. 1, p. 87, Paris, 1967.) It is probable that the manna of John's tomb was the equivalent of that from the *murabits* of Moslem saints in North Africa and elsewhere, and similarly credited with therapeutic properties. For *mana*, or indwelling power of material objects, see Norman Cohn, *The Pursuit of the Millennium*, London, 1957, p. 50.

The tomb of St John is still shown at Selçuk but is now in an underground passage to which access is denied. There is a fine new marble tomb at present ground level, part of the reconstruction of the basilica by the Friends of Ephesus of Lima, Ohio, U.S.A.

Even in Muntaner's day the tomb of St Demetrius, patron of Thessalonika, exuded a magic oil which effected wonderful cures in those who approached it with faith (Anna Comnena, *The Alexiad*, London, 1969, p. 93, n. 27).

Chapter 4

1 Muntaner devotes only one short chapter to this tremendous march. Some authorities deny that it ever took place, but the majority credit the tale.

2 The ruins of Hierapolis and the strange cliffs of Pamukkale are now a tourist attraction and, horrible to relate, five motels have been built among the ruins.

3 Op. cit., ch. 208.

4 Nicolau d'Olwer, *L'Expansio*, sect. 22. Moncada, *Expedición*, ch. 18.

5 Merriman, *The Rise of the Spanish Empire*, ch. 8.

6 Pachymeres, *Histoire de Constantinople*, 12, ch. 2.

7 Moncada, op. cit., ch. 23.

8 Muntaner wrote that the resounding title of Caesar had been in abeyance for 400 years. According to Pears, *The Destruction*, p. 43, the title had become greatly cheapened by the beginning of the thirteenth century. Certainly the

history of its devaluation was a long one, going back to at least the ninth century (Bréhier, *Instituciones,* ch. 1, sect. 5).

9 This is Muntaner's phrase; the palm is still the official measure of land in Catalonia.

10 Nicolau d'Olwer, op. cit., sect. 23.

11 Pachymeres, op. cit., 12, ch. 2.

12 Moncada, op. cit., ch. 22.

Chapter 5

1 Op. cit., ch. 215.

2 Pachymeres, *Histoire de Constantinople,* vol. 2, 6, ch. 24. There is doubt regarding her names. The meticulous Rubió i Lluch, for instance, calls her Maria Xena ('La Companyia').

3 Book 8, ch. 3.

4 *L'Expansio,* sect. 24.

5 He was later deposed by his grandson after a prolonged and ruinous civil war.

6 E.g. Merriman, op. cit., *passim.*

7 Maria gave birth to a posthumous son, Rogeron, who was twenty years old when Muntaner began to write his chronicle, *Cronica* (ch. 213).

8 Pachymeres, op. cit., vol. 2, 5, ch. 12.

9 Rubió i Ors.

10 An earlier embassy, complaining about arrears of pay, is mentioned in great detail by Moncada, *Expedición,* ch. 28. Its three members are named and are not identical with any of Siscar's party.

11 Muntaner, *Cronica,* ch. 215.

Chapter 6

1 Moncada, *Expedición,* ch. 33.

2 The Catalan version of *hyperperi,* the latest name for what had been the gold *solidus* of Constantine I and later the *nomisma* and the *bezant.* It is difficult to assess the values in terms of purchasing power, but at today's prices the original *solidus* may have been worth $10 U.S. and the *hyperpre* of Andronicus II about $1.

3 Muntaner, *Cronica,* ch. 219.

4 Moncada, op. cit., ch. 34.

5 Ibid., ch. 35.

6 Pachymeres, *Histoire de Constantinople,* 6, ch. 32.

7 Muntaner, op. cit., ch. 221.

8 Pachymeres, op. cit., 6, chap. 33.

9 In 1259 the Byzantine army under Michael VIII Palaeologos, father of Andronicus II, defeated the Frankish chivalry at Pelagonia, in western Macedonia. In Michael's army were 500 Turkish mercenaries. See Miller, *The Latins in the Levant,* p. 111.

10 Stewart, D., *Great Cairo,* London, 1969.

Chapter 7

1 An insight into the devastation and terror that obtained in the area close to the Catalan camps. Few medieval forces in hostile territory would send out unarmed foraging parties.

2 He must have obtained the facts at second hand, for he had been left in charge at Gallipoli.

3 It was the custom for foreign brides of Byzantine royalty to take a Greek name on their marriage.

4 Muntaner, *Cronica,* ch. 227.

5 Muntaner uses the word *tinyoso*: afflicted with ringworm. The English translation of Lady Goodenough is difficult to accept: *tres* here probably means 'trash' or 'rabble', rather than 'three'.

6 Another adventurous Catalan, who had travelled through Armenia to Persia as ambassador of James II of Aragón.

7 Pachymeres, cited by Nicolau d'Olwer, *L'Expansio*, sect. 27.

8 Possibly Muntaner recalled that Ticino's uncle Benedetto, an earlier Zaccaria, had been brother-in-law of Peter III of Aragón; the family that leased Chios from the Byzantines cannot have suffered excessively from the alleged excesses of the Catalan fleet in the winters of 1302 and 1303.

9 New Phocaea was not far to the north-east of classical Phocaea (Foça), north of Smyrna (Izmir) on the west coast of Asia Minor. It grew up round the castle on the sea-shore, built to guard the valuable alum mines; in the days of Genoese ownership it was successively known as Fogia and Folia, whence it figures as the mysterious Fuylla in Muntaner's chronicle.

Today it keeps its name in the small seaside resort of Yenifoça; the sole visible remnant of the Genoese castle rises as a crumbling block of masonry a few yards offshore. Other remnants can be seen underwater and most of the nearby houses are built of large stone blocks.

10 The True Cross had been brought from Jerusalem, where it had been discovered by Constantine's mother, the Empress Helena, to Constantinople at the time of the Arab conquests in the seventh century. It was kept in the royal palace and almost immediately partitioned into splinters, which were given freely to sanctuaries, monasteries and foreign potentates. Their retail price fluctuated, but at this time was still considerable.

11 The family of Zaccaria still exists in Anatolia under the name of Zakariyeh. One of its living representatives in Izmir had discovered its Genoese origin but knew nothing of its connection with Yenifoça until informed of this by the present writer.

Chapter 8

1 Manzano, *Los Grandes,* p. 44.

2 Rubió, 'La Companyia . . .' *Miscellanea Prat de la Riba,* p. 224.

3 *Expedición,* ch. 50.

4 *Histoire de Constantinople,* 7, ch. 34. Muntaner (*Cronica,* chs 225, 231) points out that the Company never dug or planted.

5 We must bear in mind that gentle birth had nothing to do with gentle behaviour. Entenza was an enthusiastic practitioner of the Catalan Vengeance and long before that a participant in the terrible raids of his brother-in-law, Roger de Lluria.

6 Op. cit., ch. 235.

7 Miller, *The Latins in the Levant,* p. 217.

8 The frescoes which decorated every available interior wall were famous, as

were the gatherings at Thebes of the Frankish chivalry, whose splendour outshone that of France and Burgundy, whence they had sprung (Miller, op. cit., p. 264).

9 It became the custom to prefix the name of a city with the preposition εἰς, which took the meaning 'at'. Thus Thebes became εἰς τὰς Θῆβας (eis tas Thevas) and so Estives; Athens εἰς τὰς 'Αθῆνας, Sathines or Cetines; the hermitages of Meteora εἰς τοὺς 'άγιους, (eis tous hagious—at the holy men), Stagious. Constantinople, *the* city, εἰς τὴν πόλιν (eis ten polin), thus achieving its eventual name of Istanbul or Stamboul.

10 Moncada, op. cit., ch. 56.

11 He could not have known that the acquisition of Byzantium had been the aim of Frederick II of Sicily for some years. See p. 95 above.

12 As previously stated, Muntaner himself was never indemnified for his loss. In 1356 Muntaner's granddaughter brought an action, in Venice, against the descendants of John Teri and Mark Miyot (in Muntaner's spelling), the Venetian captains who had despoiled the *Española*. She was awarded 11,000 gold florins, which is estimated at about ten per cent of the 25,000 ounces of gold of which her grandfather had been robbed. In 1304 the gold ounce was equivalent to five florins. The document of 31 August 1307, which is shortly to be mentioned, no doubt helped her considerably. For details see Predelli, *I Libri Commemoriali, 1,* 87; *2,* 186, 190, 250; cited by Miller, op. cit., p. 217.

13 Op. cit., ch. 238.

14 He is believed to have lived for at least ten years after beginning to write his famous chronicle at the age of sixty; he died on the Island of Ibiza. His chronicle has been a source of knowledge and inspiration to generations of historians and, not surprisingly, of at least one romance of chivalry. *Tirant lo Blanch,* written in Catalan in 1460, recounts the adventures of a western hero summoned to Constantinople, which he saved from the Turks. The Princess Carmesina is bestowed on him in marriage and he achieves the dignity of a Caesar. His companions, of the House of Rocasalada, attain such illustrious posts as High Admiral, Grand Constable and Duke of Macedonia. The romance is a thinly disguised account of Roger de Flor and his captains, written when the only record of their adventures was to be found in Muntaner's chronicle.

15 Villehardouin, *Memoirs of the Crusades,* intro., p. xxii.

Chapter 9

1 Rubió, 'La Companyia . . .' *Miscellanea Prat del Riba,* pp. 220 et seq. Muntaner, *Cronica,* ch. 239.

2 Rubió 'Los Navarros . . .' *Mem. Real Acad. Buenas Letras,* p. 365. Muntaner, op. cit., ch. 239.

3 See note 1.

4 See note 1.

5 Rubió i Lluch assumes that either Roger's daughter had died or that the wedding had never taken place.

6 Her name was the official one assumed on marriage. She was really Yolande, daughter of the Marquis of Montferrat and as ambitious as other members of that house.

7 Thessalonika had in fact been captured only twice, once by the Saracens in the tenth century and again in 1182 by the Normans of Sicily.

8 Daniel II nevertheless describes repeated attacks by the Catalan Company. See note 1.

9 The title of Grand Duke, used by Frankish chroniclers, is the result of a pardonable error; they were led astray by his family name being Ducas.

10 Their usual procedure was to slaughter the adults and keep the children, whom they brought up to be either servants or soldiers; the practice was not peculiar to the Catalans, who possibly had in mind the example of the Mamelukes of Egypt. There the use of slaves brought up to be soldiers had since 1254 transferred all power into the hands of the 'captives'; the Ottoman Turks were to recruit their janissaries in the same way. The Catalan custom was therefore in the best oriental tradition. I know of no similar practice in Catalonia, Spain or Sicily and it was therefore probably adopted during their expedition to the east.

11 The first part of the life of Athanasios continued to be restless; after leaving the Company—we do not know when or how—he visited Crete and Constantinople and is next heard of on Mt Athos, where he received the tonsure in 1335. From there he and nine other monks fled to avoid the menace of Turkish pirates and, wandering in the region of his old home, picked on the rock of Doupiani; it was later called 'celestial', or 'Meteora', for its strange configuration promised security. The Church of the Transfiguration still preserves the title of the original monastery's dedication, and the chosen site proved its worth for five centuries, until at last it was sacked by brigands in 1831. The village of Stagious, just to the south, took its name from the Meteorites, as previously explained.

12 I have not had the opportunity of consulting this work, edited and published by Constantine N. Sathas, Athens, 1865. It seems hopeless to try to reconcile the inconsistencies of the Galaxidi Chronicle, which may be reporting an earlier episode, before the recall of Chalandrinos.

13 Although some of the Almugavars are known to have come from Tarragona the word is a corruption of 'Aragonese'.

14 One of the many names met in the transition from Naupaktos to Lepanto.

15 "Ωστ' ᾄδουσι μὲν ἐς δεῦρο Θετταλοί ᾄδουσῖ δέ σχεδόν πάντες ἄνθρωποι. Cited by Rubió, *Expedición*, p. 17. The relevant epistle of Theodulos was translated into Spanish by Gaspar Santiñón, *Rev. Cienc. hist.* No. 1, April, 1880.

16 When the French took the phrase over, only too literally, they changed the German *Moment* into a period of time and we have copied it without question as a paraphrase for 'the critical instant'.

Chapter 10

1 See ch. 1 for the same title bestowed on Roger de Flor, and Miller, *The Latins in the Levant*, p. 107.

2 '*Arena* [*Helena—A.L.*] wife of the Duke of Athens . . .' with the usual medieval ignorance of classical history.

3 *Cronica*, ch. 244.

4 Muntaner, op. cit., ch. 240.

5 Gregoras, *A History of Greece* (See Migne), 7, ch. 7. It is interesting to

observe how the image of the Company improves when the Catalans are no longer fighting against Byzantium.

6 Because they had fought for Ferdinand II of Sicily.

7 Nicolau d'Olwer, *L'Expansio*, sect. 33.

8 Thomas, *Diplomatorium Veneto–Levantinum* (Monumenti storici), Venice, Deputazione veneta di storia patria, 1880, p. 83.

9 Frazer, J. G., *Folk Lore of the Old Testament*, abridged ed., p. 71, London, 1923.

10 Graves, R., *The Greek Myths*, vol. 2, 198, and p. 99 n. 2, London, second edn, 1960.

11 *Livre de la Conquête*, or *Chronica metrica de Morea* was published by Buchon in the revised ed. of *Recherches historiques sur la principauté française de Morea et ses hautes baronnies*, *1*, 6 et seq. Cited by Rubió 'La Expedición . . .' *Mem. Real Acad. Buenas Letras*, p. 35.

12 The Turcopoles, whom I have mentioned several times, were the offspring of Turkish fathers and Greek mothers. In typical oriental fashion, still observed by Jews, children took their mother's religion, at least nominally.

13 Op. cit., ch. 240.

14 St Martin of Tours was a patron of French Crusaders. William of Villehardouin, Prince of Achaia, obtained from the sainted Louis IX of France the privilege of minting *tournois* in the Castle of Chloumoutsi, hence called Castel Tornese by the Italians. The coins carried a representation of the Church of St Martin at Tours and the inscription *De Clarencia*. The latter was a Latin rendering of their capital at Glarentsa; the English dukedom of Clarence is *not* derived from this, though it is tempting to place the origin of a well-known duke in the same country as the malmsey wine in which he drowned. St Martin, perhaps because he was a cavalryman, was a favourite of the French knights in the east, and an ingenious scholar has cited the war-cry '*Mihi et Beati Martino*' as the origin of our 'All my eye and Betty Martin'. To put themselves under his protection, departing pilgrims were in the habit of nailing a horseshoe to the door of St Martin's church.

Epilogue

1 The same who had sent his cousin Ferdinand of Mallorca to be their commander.

2 '*tamquam Christi verus athleta et fidelis pugio Ecclesiae*', Rubió, 'La Grecia . . .' *Inst. d'Estudis Univ. Catalans*, p. 436.

3 The Catalans are not only law-abiding but democratic. As early as 1259 they had issued the first code of maritime laws, the *Consulat del Mar*.

4 Miller, *The Latins in the Levant*, p. 244, makes Frederick II of Sicily sign this truce with Venice. We do not know whether he had authority to act for his son William, the Duke of Athens.

5 E.g. by Merriman, *The Rise of the Spanish Empire*.

6 In 1331. Rubió, op. cit., p. 436.

7 δόλοι καταλάνοι or σκύλοι καταλάνοι? See Rubió, 'La Expedición...' *Mem. Real Acad. Buenas Letras,* p. 39, footnote.

8 Rubió, op. cit., p. 436.

9 Rubió, 'Els Governs . . .', op. cit.

10 Various tales of the Last Count of Salona aroused Greek patriotism during the War of Independence in the last century, though they maligned the Catalans more than the Turks.

11 John Cantacuzenos reigned from 1347 to 1355, when he retired to the Monastery of Mangana, thoroughly disgusted with political life. During the next thirty-six years he wrote his memoirs, of which the best edition is said to be the Venetian 'Corpus bizantinae historiae Joannis Cantacuzeni eximperatoris historiarum libri IV', 1729.

12 One of the few Greek towns that preserve relics of Catalan rule, in its Spanish dances on feast days, e.g. the *trata*.

13 Miller, op. cit., p. 302.

14 Rubió, 'Els Governs . . .', op. cit., p. 15.

15 Ibid., p. 57.

16 For the full history of this band and its impact on Catalan possessions, see Rubió, 'Los Navarros . . .' *Mem. Real Acad. Buenas Letras*, passim.

17 His tombstone may be seen in the infirmary ward of the Knights' Hospital in Rhodes.

18 G. Kambouroglou, *Hai Pallaiai Athenai*, Athens 1922, pp. 144–6, showed that the fresco was painted in the fifteenth century, probably at the expense of the Genoese. The Italian origin was confirmed by L. J. A. Loewenthal, *Athens Annals of Archaeology* 4, 89, 1971.

Sources

Such is the wealth of books and articles dealing with the Levant from the fourth Crusade to the Turkish conquest, that only a few of the leading authorities are indicated here. The task of analysis and presentation was first undertaken by Buchon in the first half of the nineteenth century. Among his works was the French translation of Ramón Muntaner's chronicle and various editions of the *Livre de la Conquête*, the anonymous chronicle of the Franks in the Morea; the best of four manuscripts of this work came to light in Copenhagen in 1845 and made a new edition of Buchon's work imperative.

Hopf, at about the middle of the century, was equally productive and is still a source of much information. Finlay's history follows similar lines. Fuller knowledge of the Catalan Company stems from two sources: the study of coins and seals by Schlumberger, and the intensive, nay devoted, studies of the great Catalan historian Rubió i Lluch over more than fifty years, beginning in the 1880s. Much of his contribution arises from close study of the Archives of the Crown of Aragón, previously an almost untapped source. By listing his works I have found it unnecessary to cite some earlier authors, such as Ducange and Zurita.

The most complete summary in English is undoubtedly that of William Miller, who gives to the Catalans a little over two chapters of the eighteen that describe the rise and fall of the Latins in the Levant. As mentioned in the foreword, there is no single book dealing exclusively with the Catalan Company during and after its days of conquest. Miller's classic comes nearest to supplying the facts.

The following list is to be taken as an introductory guide. The Byzantine authorities, who are in the main biased by personal or patriotic considerations, are included, though their accounts of the Catalans are often unreliable. The same, of course, applies conversely to Moncada's book.

An asterisk indicates works available only in Catalan.

BRÉHIER, L. L., *La Civilizacion Bizantina*, Mexico, 1955.
Las Instituciones del Imperio Bizantino, Mexico, 1956.
Vida y Muerte de Bizancio, Mexico, 1956. (All translated from the French by J. Almoina.)

CANTACUZENE, J., *Corpus bizantinae historiae*, 4 vols, Venice, 1729.

*DESCLOT, B., *Crónica del Rey En Pere*, Barcelona, 1885.

FERMOR, P. L., *Roumeli*, London, 1966 (for the history of Athanasios the Meteorite).

FINLAY, G., *A History of Greece*, vol. 4, Oxford, 1877.

HOPF, *Griechenland im Mittelalter und in der Neuzeit*, Leipzig, 1870.

MANZANO, R., *Los Grandes Capitanes Españoles*, Barcelona, 1960.

MERRIMAN, R. B., *The Rise of the Spanish Empire*, vol. 1, ch. 8, p. 363, New York, 1962.

MIGNE, J. P., *Patrologia graeca*, for Nikephoros Gregoras: vol. 148; for George Pachymeres: vol. 144 (in Latin and Greek); for Phrantzes: vol. 156.

MILLER, W., *The Latins in the Levant*, Cambridge, 1964 edn.

MONCADA, F. DE, *Expedición de los Catalanes y Aragoneses contra Turcos y Griegos*, Buenos Aires, 1948.

MUNTANER, R., *Crónica*, Barcelona, 1886. English translation by Lady Goodenough, London, 1920.

*NICOLAU D'OLWER, L., *L'Expansio de Catalunya an la Mediterrània Oriental*, Barcelona, 1926.

PACHYMERES, GEORGE, *Histoire de Constantinople* (French trans. Cousin), vol. 6, Paris, 1673.

PAYNE, R., *The Splendours of Greece*, London, 1960 (on the relics of St George).

PEARS, E., *The Destruction of the Greek Empire and the Story of the Capture of Constantinople by the Turks*, London, 1903.

RODD, SIR RENNELL, *The Princes of Achaia and the Chronicles of Morea*, 2 vols, London, 1907.

RUBIÓ I LLUCH, A., 'La Expedición y Dominación de los Catalanes en Oriente juzgados por los Griegos', *Mem. Real Acad. Buenas Letras*, *4, 5*, Barcelona, 1883.
'Los Navarros en Grecia y el Ducado Catalán de Atenas en la Época de su Invasión, ibid., *4*, 223, Barcelona, 1886.
*'Atenes en temps dels Catalans', *Inst. d'Estudis Catalans*, 225, 1907.
*'La població dels ducats catalans de Grècia', *Bol. Real Acad. Buenas Letras de Barcelona*, *4*, 489, 1908.
*'Els Castells Catalans de la Grècia continental', *Inst. d'Estudis Univ. Catalans*, 364, 1908.
*'Els Governs de Mattheu de Moncada y Roger de Lluria en la Grècia Catalana', ibid., *3*, 1911–12.
*'Contribució a la biografia de l'infant Ferran de Mallorca', ibid., *7*, 291, 1913.
*'La Grecia Catalana des de la mort de Roger de Lluria fins a la de Federico III de Sicilia', ibid., 393, 1913–14.
*'La Grecia Catalana des de la mort de Federico III fins a la invasió Navarresa', ibid., 156, 1915–20.

*'La Companyia Catalana sóta el comandament de Teobald de Cepoy', *Miscellanea Prat de la Riba*, *1*, 219 (Inst. d'Est. Catal.), 1919.

*'Per què diem Catalana a la nostra Dominació a Grècia?', ibid., *12*, 1 1927.

*'La Població de la Grècia Catalana en el XIV Segle', ibid., *Memòries de la Secció Historico-Arqueologica*, *4*, Barcelona, 1933.

RUNCIMAN, S., *A History of the Crusades*, 3 vols, London, 1954.

SCHLUMBERGER, G., *Expédition des Almugavares ou routiers Catalans en Orient de l'an 1302 à l'an 1311*, Paris, 1902.

Scéaux des Feudatoires et du Clergé de l'Empire Latin de Constantinople, Caen, 1898.

THEODULUS MAGISTER, cited by Rubió, 'La Expedición de los Catalanes en Oriente juzgados por los Griegos', ch. 4.

VASILIEV, A. A., *Historia del Imperio Bizantino*. Trans. from French by J. G. de Luaces, 2 vols, Barcelona, 1946.

VILLEHARDOUIN, G., *Memoirs of the Crusades,* with Introduction by Sir Frank Marzials, London, 1908.

Index

Index